The
Colour
Source
Book

THE COLOUR SOURCE BOOK

Margaret Walch

With 246 colour samples
and 48 black-and-white illustrations

Thames and Hudson

First published in Great Britain in 1979
by Thames and Hudson Ltd, London

Copyright © 1971 Margaret S. Walch and American Fabrics Magazine

Printed and bound in the USA

CONTENTS

COLOR SOURCE BOOK CHARTS

FOREWORD

This is essentially an historical color sourcebook for artists, designers, and craftsmen. Beginning with the colors found on the tombs of Ancient Egypt and ending with an American Pop Art Palette of the 1960's, the book focuses on the highpoints in color expression throughout history. Special attention is paid to the palettes of great painters and to the way in which they were used to achieve unusual chromatic effects.

The AF Color Sourcebook carefully illustrates its chosen themes. From four to eight characteristic colors have been selected for each period, work of art, or artist. These colors do not presume to represent the actual pigments used. Rather, they have been chosen on a visual basis. They can be thought of as key colors for a particular artist, work of art, or period and so they form a distinctive basic palette with historical authenticity.

The text accompanying each group of colors is intended to explain why certain colors have been chosen and how they were used to achieve unusual color effects within works of art. Also, the text seeks to elucidate how technical problems (like the use of glazes in porcelain or varnishes in the works of old masters) very often led to brilliant chromatic solutions.

For the painters' palettes shown in this portfolio, some explanation is required. Of course, it is presumptuous to think of distilling the essence of a great painter's multi-hued palette in five or six color swatches. Most of them used the full spectrum of pigment available in their time. Nevertheless, color being so personal a sensation, each painter favored some hues and combinations over others. Indeed, such colors are often the ones which create the dominant impression we carry away with us after viewing a painting. These are the colors which have been carefully isolated out of the much larger spectrum of the artist's total achievement.

Although more than half of this book deals with pre-nineteenth century art, its material is relevant to contemporary times. As man learns more and more to control his surroundings, his concern for the quality of that environment grows more pressing. From the caveman's paintings on, color has played a key role in determining the emotional as well as the aesthetic responses of man to his environment.

Today, a fantastic number of choices made by a diverse body of people have a very real impact on our every waking moment. Someone else, someone "out there" decides the range of colors available for the telephone on your desk, the ink in your pen, the fabric of your shirt. Someone "out there" is the audience for this book — the men and women who choose the colors which enhance our common environment and give it vitality.

This book could not have come into being without the full cooperation of the Staff of American Fabrics and Fashions Magazine and their research facilities. My debt also must be acknowledged to the staffs of the Art and Architecture Library of Yale University and of the Metropolitan Museum of Art.

MARGARET WALCH

INTRODUCTION

George Orwell selected the year 1984 as the setting for his novel about a totalitarian, mechanized, de-personalized society. At one time this seemed a date — and a prediction — comfortably removed from the present. But it is now upon us.

The eternal struggle between life-giving and death-dealing forces intensifies in scope, widens in implication from individual man to our entire race. Two thousand, even one thousand years ago, man could only bring destruction upon that which he could physically touch. Now we are faced not only with potential devastation by awesome weapons at a great distance, but with the even more insidious perils of an unwittingly polluted atmosphere in which one casualty of ecological imbalance may someday be man himself.

These are by no means new ideas, but what is new is the extent to which they are permeating the consciousness of our entire race. The select few who once joined battle against unhealthy foods and dangerous air have now been augmented by vast armies of people the world over. "Bigger," "faster," "standardized" — these words no longer mean "better" to a new awakened public. This public now wants to improve the quality of life, not the quantity of material trappings which surround us.

*   *   *

A CASE IN POINT for this change in attitude may be found in the allied worlds of art and fashion. In the mid-19th century, the brilliant feats of chemistry by Perkins and his followers created synthetic color dyes. Man could and did create a limitless variety of colors, with infinite combinations and permutations. Only now we sense that this was not an unmixed blessing. Before these discoveries, the artist-colorist had to assemble colors painstakingly according to the natural laws of their suitability to specific media, while bearing in mind the interactions of various organic compounds. Even the stuffs from which colors are derived could only be achieved by toil and ingenuity. We moderns, on the other hand, because we have had such easy access to a world of color not readily available in other times, have been, to put it mildly, rather cavalier in our employment of color. Too often we use color and color combinations rather lightly, neither respecting experience nor making the effort to study the principles and motivations behind their selections. Perhaps because color today is omni-present and because so many shades of color are easily accessible, we need more discipline, more care in understanding root meanings and in understanding aesthetic considerations as well.

WHICH BRINGS US to this book by Margaret Walch, who has researched and assembled a history of significant color palettes from all the civilizations of the world, ranging back to pre-historic man and right up to the present day. Several of these palettes were created by individual artists, such as El Greco, Rubens, Van Gogh, and Matisse. More are the collective product of anonymous craftsmen working through time to establish the most beautiful, most "correct" combinations of colors for such media as Chinese porcelain, Greek vases, African masks and batik fabrics.

Margaret Walch's research has implications which go beyond the cataloguing of a series of historically accurate, painstakingly reproduced color palettes. Her book serves to remind us how important it is that we do not ignore the great heritage which the different families of the race have bequeathed us. Every epoch, every civilization has made its own unique contribution to the common pool. Our modern technology, in many respects serving the betterment of society, has had the dangerous side effect of severing some life-giving lines to our rich and more natural past.

We must not forget that those men — both the famous artists and the anonymous craftsmen — who originated these palettes did not make their color selection by chance or by whim. When the race was younger, we were closer to nature. We could hear, and see, and feel, and understand her predilections in a much more direct way.

And this is perhaps as important an aspect of this work on color as the palettes themselves. For she goes beyond or, perhaps better, behind the colors briefly to describe those forces which led to their original selection. No artist, no man, makes decisions in a vacuum. For these palettes, aesthetic considerations were of course paramount. But almost as important were other kinds of forces operating upon the artist — the practical limits of dyes, the social responses of his chosen audience, even philosophical beliefs about the significance of various colors.

To take but one example from Margaret Walch's book, in the painting of African masks the presence or absence of certain hues, and the way they are juxtaposed and combined, mean certain very specific things to the audience for whom they are intended. And the same is true of a medieval manuscript illumination, a Persian miniature page, a Van Gogh painting, or a piece of oriental porcelain. Precious lapis-lazuli blue, for example, was reserved by medieval painters for coloring the robes of Christ and the Madonna, and the Tibetans reserved the color gold for the Dalai Lama.

THIS IS NOT TO SAY that we must arbitrarily adhere to ancient rules and follow these palettes in every particular, True, they are guides, perhaps as authentic as have ever been assembled. But the author is not suggesting an unnecessarily purist approach. It would be too limiting to insist that next to celadon green may be placed only those limited hues specified by the Chinese artists of the ancient dynasties. New palettes are constantly being invented to supplement the old. New masters — Matisse, for example — arrive in each epoch to equal those of past centuries in their understanding of the potential of color and in their appliance and instinct for the color juste. At any point in time it is important, however, that we do understand the past before we try to make it over in our own image as we hurry on our way to the future.

This, again, is a concept whose significance is now appreciated the world over. The age of one culture arrogantly imposing its values upon another is, happily, drawing to a close. The age of wishing all cultures to conform to one particular standard of behavior, one particular standard of taste now seems more like a nightmare than a dream. Complexity, not sameness. Wonderment, not absolute knowledge. These are the keynotes of the new sensibility. Henry Ford once told his customers they could have any color automobile they wanted so long as it was black. His grandson now presides over a corporation that acknowledges the significance of individual taste.

What does this all mean to an audience for a book of historically important combinations of colors. Simply a gentle word of advice. In looking at these palettes, perhaps in using them as sources of inspiration for contemporary design, the best approach is not one that comes god-like from above, but one that tries to look through the eyes of the people who created them. Sympathy and understanding. Old-fashioned virtues, perhaps. But contemporary, too. They were quite obviously a vital element in the creation of this book. May they be part of its use — and users — as well.

WILLIAM C. SEGAL

CHINESE PORCELAIN COLORS

WITH the establishment of the peace-loving Sung Dynasty (960-1276), the "Augustan Age" of Chinese history began. During the Sung Dynasty porcelain was manufactured for the first time on a large scale. The keenest artistic perception and a rare technical development distinguish Sung specimens. Lovely buff shades, soft cream white, harsh bluish white, biscuit hues—these are the colors in the earliest examples of Sung porcelain. Céladon is usually given the place of honor in the Sung period. Under the generic name céladon one finds many shades of green displaying various tones of olive, together with colors that recall young grass in full sunlight and the various shades of mineral jade.

In striking contrast to the céladon glazes, which are cool and rootful in tone, are the infinite variety of red glazes which display every tone from pink to the deep aubergine of the Ming Dynasty (1368-1644). Notable colors of the Ming period are Sang de Boeuf, a brilliant red glaze, which exhibits patches like coagulated ox blood, cucumber green, and apple green. All these colors owe their effects to different combinations of glazes and underglazes.

The virtuosity of Chinese artists in creating porcelain colors has astounded people for centuries. We know how the Chinese achieved some of their more startling color effects. Powder blue was made by blowing powdered cobalt through a bamboo tube onto a surface; then glaze was applied over it, thus producing the mottled effect. Nankin blue, often seen on blue and white Chinese porcelain, was made from salt of cobalt. When highly petrified, it gave a deep brilliant blue; when less processed, it produced a grayish tone. Yet, even today, mystery still surrounds much of the art of Chinese porcelain colors.

Ming Red

Pale Apple

Tang Green

Sung Blue

Cucumber Green

Deep Apple

COLORS IN CALICO PRINTING

FOR 2000 years or more, the history of India has been closely bound up with her pre-eminence as producer of textiles. The influence of Indian textiles on the English-speaking world is revealed in such names as calico, madras, muslin, shawl, sash, pajamas, gingham, dungaree, bandanna, chintz, khaki.

India is the home of cotton. Printing and painting of cotton are the art for which Indian textiles have long been famed abroad. Until as late as the seventeenth century, the Indians alone had mastered the complicated chemistry of cotton dyeing, which presents technical problems that do not occur in the dyeing of non-vegetable fibers like silk and wool.

The name Calico is derived from the small town of Calicut, where cotton was first printed, and not from the city of Calcutta as is popularly believed. The colors are not bright, but they are resonant like the tones of deep glowing jewels. The old "patterned Calicoes" had reds ranging from crimson to delicate shell pink, and purple tones from the deepest violet to the palest lavender. There was also an indigo blue and a lemon yellow. It is strange that from such a vigorously colored textile the modern version of the single-hued calicoes should have evolved.

Two of the calico colors in our palette are turkey red, a lavender red, and Indian red, a brownish red. Both are typical of madder-dyed and resist-printed cottons of Indian saris made 200 years ago. Also chosen are a sage-green and an indigo blue. These colors have been perennial favorites in cotton fabrics.

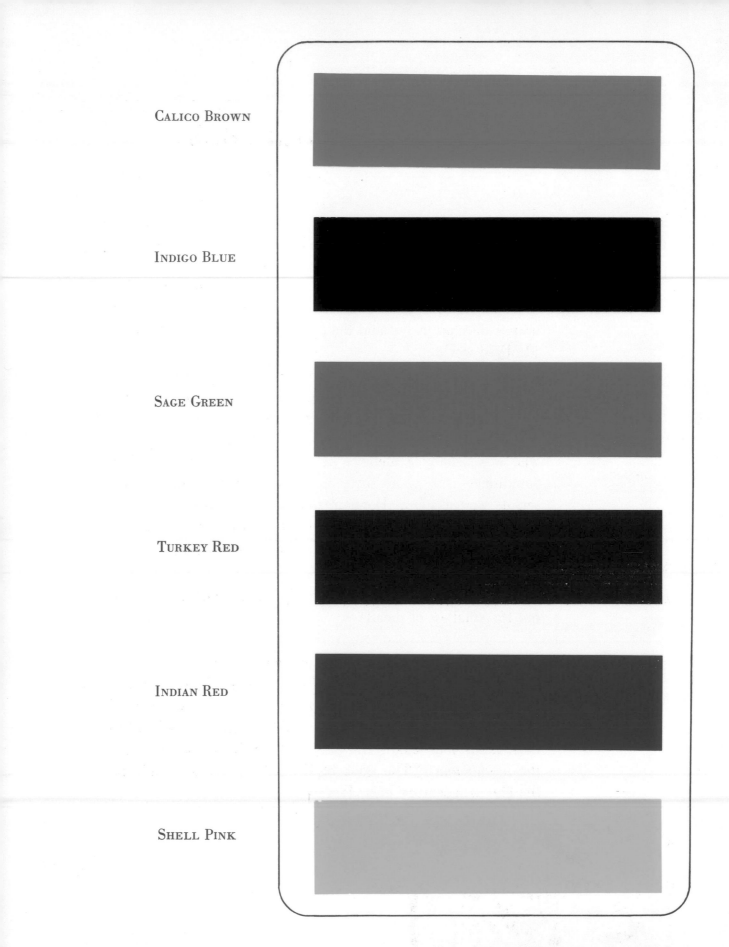

CALICO BROWN

INDIGO BLUE

SAGE GREEN

TURKEY RED

INDIAN RED

SHELL PINK

PERSIAN MINIATURE COLORS

PERSIAN miniature painting is primarily the art of book illustration, for the Persian miniature invariably tells a story. Since the Persian artists drew not from nature but according to accepted artistic convention, the figures and landscapes they portrayed and the colors they used came from an idealized world.

Perfection of materials marks the Persian miniature. The fine, smoothly-polished paper, the costly, pure pigments, and the lavish gold, all demanded a wealthy and enlightened patron who was usually a member of a ruling house. Prince Baysunghur — for whom some of the finest illuminated manuscripts were made at Herat in the early fifteenth century — maintained a staff of 40 for their production, including calligraphers, painters, illuminators, gilders and binders.

Flatly applied to accord with the page format and the calligraphy, the jewel-like pigments of Persian miniatures pick out the smallest of details.

The most frequent color combination was a gold ground and a blue sky. Three shades of Persian blue — a deep azure, a grey-green blue, and a pale white blue — and two tints of gold — a pale yellow and a deep gold — are all used in the most sumptuous manuscript produced for Prince Baysunghur, the *Shah-nama* ("The Book of Kings"), a national epic by the eleventh-century poet Firdawsi.

BOKARA BLUE

COTTON BLUE

ORANGE

SHAH GOLD

PERSIAN TURQUOISE

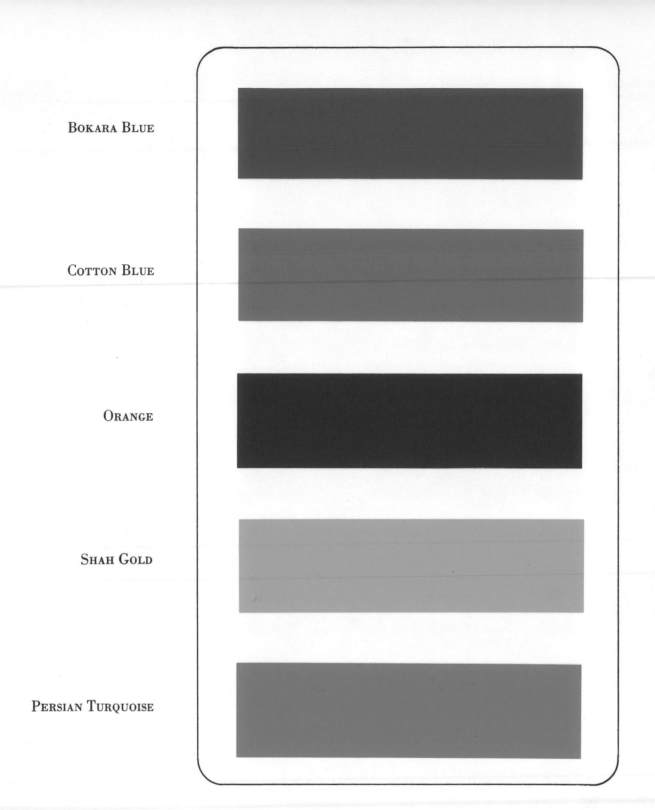

FOR 3000 years, covering 30 dynasties, the Pharaonic artists in the Nile Valley produced masterpieces which delighted the eye. Despite the ravages of time, a sufficient number of Pharaonic paintings have survived to give us a fairly accurate idea of the range of colors employed in the tempera process, which was used exclusively.

The ochres — red, yellow and brown — were mostly used for flesh tints. Blue for backgrounds and green for foliage, enameled beads, etc. were derived from copper frit (calcinated material used in glass making). Black, derived from soot, invariably used for the stylized wigs that characterized Egyptian women, was also mixed with white to produce a soft grey.

Starting with the Rameses epoch (XIII-XII centuries B.C.), yellow began to replace blue as a background color and a much more vivid palette, including pinks and roses, bright blues and greens, was used.

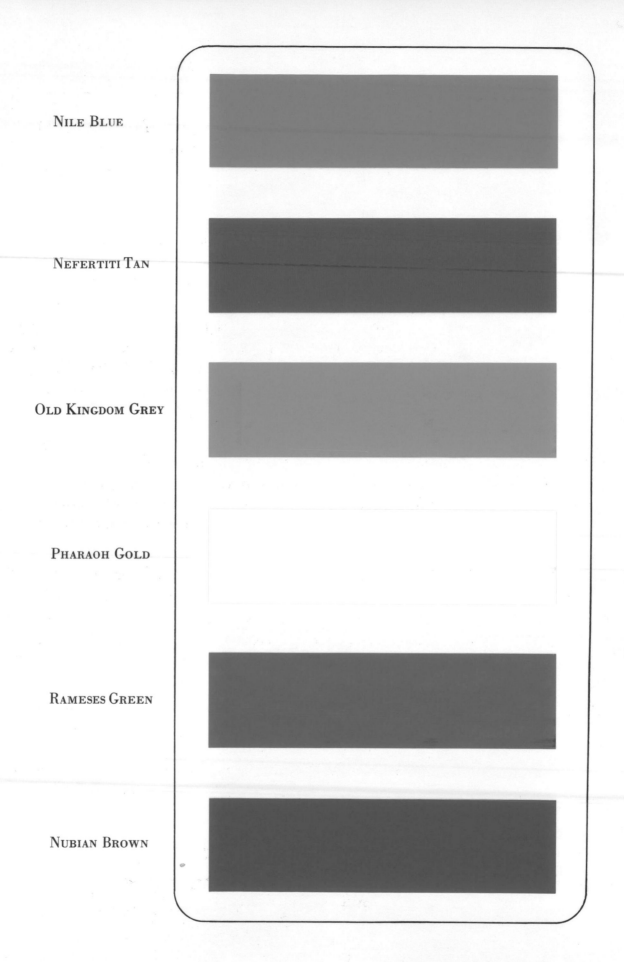

NILE BLUE

NEFERTITI TAN

OLD KINGDOM GREY

PHARAOH GOLD

RAMESES GREEN

NUBIAN BROWN

ANCIENT PERUVIAN TEXTILE COLORS
INCA (PRE-COLUMBIAN)

WEAVING was the outstanding craft of Ancient Peru. With native cotton and wool from the domesticated llama and alpaca and the wild vicuña, the Ancient Peruvians practised every technique known to handloom weavers today. Examples of embroidery, tinsel, leno, brocades like those now requiring a very modern Jacquard loom, double-cloths and even knotted net, have all been found in Ancient Peru's tombs. The Peruvians excelled in fine cotton weaving, specializing in woven patterns in contrast to the printed cotton of India.

Peruvian textiles present a wealth of harmonious colors. Besides black and white and the several natural shades of cotton and wool, as many as 190 hues have been distinguished in Ancient Peruvian textiles. Combinations of many colors — sometimes as many as twenty-two in a single fabric — are unique to Peruvian textiles.

The two great pan-Peruvian cultures, Tiahuanaco (600-900 A.D.) and Inca (1100-1530 A.D.), were noted for an exuberant use of warm color harmonies. Thanks to the extreme aridity of the climate, an accurate color record was preserved when Peruvian tombs were unearthed. In symbolic, often checkerboard patterns and motifs of puma gods (half man and half beast), birdheads, cats, llamas or fish, a recurring color harmony was composed of deep blood red, llama straw, desert-sun orange, and white. These colors predominate in the finest Tiahuanaco tapestries and the best examples of Inca ponchos. A more sparing use was made of indigo blue, turquoise, and bark brown.

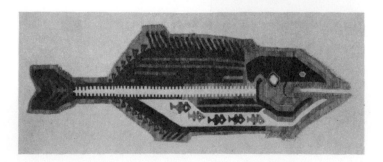

INCA BROWN

BLOOD RED

TURQUOISE

LLAMA STRAW

DESERT SUN

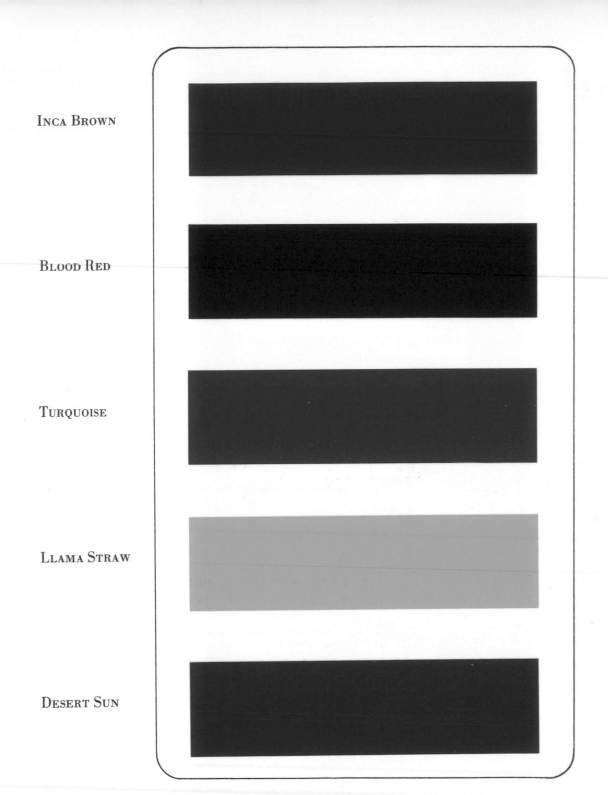

TIBETAN COLORS

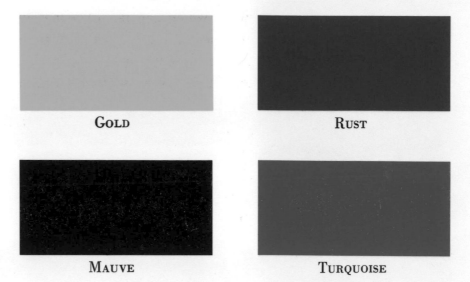

GOLD

RUST

MAUVE

TURQUOISE

THIS STRANGE land on top of the world is noted for its symbolism and religion. But it also has a symbolism of color, with key colors having special significance. The Tibetans not only invented a language of color but a language of materials. Most of their silks come from China, but their materials, such as wool and fur, are home raised.

Everything in Tibet starts with the Lama. Almost all clothing — robes, boots and high headpiece — are of the same shade of gold, the color of highest significance for Tibetans.

The hierarchy of color, fixed for centuries, follows: gold = dignity; yellow = highest officials, dynasty; mauve, especially in brocade = highest; grey/blue = people from great estates; maroon/red = people generally. Rust and turquoise are two colors which are also widely used and appreciated in Tibet.

JAPANESE SHIBUI COLORS

"SHIBUI" is a Japanese word which can be inadequately translated as meaning quietness and elegance. The term takes historical meaning from the early Zen Chinese paintings which marked an almost contemptuous break with the ornate designs and lavish colors of the Buddhist works of art which preceded them. The great simplicity with which gradations are used in the creation of cha'an paintings (especially in the Northern Sung period; 960-1127 A.D.) is noteworthy.

Like the Chinese Zen painters, those of the Japanese school — which evolved in the 15th century — strive to still the fleeting moment. Quick, sure strokes, with no attempt at sculptural effect, snare a flying bird or freeze a foaming wave. The medium used is Chinese ink, gradated from lustrous black to subtle grey. The background is always white paper or blank silk with the blank areas representing space.

SESSHU GREY   SOAMI BEIGE

SOEN BROWN   SESSON GREEN

JAPANESE WOODCUT COLORS

SOFTLY radiant, rainbow-like colors mark the Japanese woodcuts of the late eighteenth and first half of the nineteenth century. Pale roses, oranges, blues, subdued greens, chocolate browns, greys, buffs, whites are the hues that invariably appear. The soft tones of the watercolor pigments are undoubtedly enhanced by the superb texture and surface of the handmade papers, often made from mulberry bark.

Japanese woodcuts were made originally for the middle class of artisans and shopkeepers, which grew up at the beginning of the seventeenth century in Edo (present-day Tokyo) under the stability and prosperity of the firm rule of the Tokugawa Shogunate. To cater to the new middle class taste a popular theater, the Kabuki, and a voluminous literature came into being, and woodcuts were first made as pictorial records of Kabuki stars and as book illustrations. Only later did the woodcut become a picture in its own right.

Until 1742 only black blocks were used and prints were colored by hand. In 1742 two wood blocks were first used. The favorite scheme for these two-colored prints (beniye) was a rose and green. In 1764, Suzuki Harunobu invented the full color print (nishiki-ye or brocade print).

Until the late nineteenth century, colors of Japanese woodcuts were mainly of vegetable origin. Unfortunately fugitive on exposure to light, the sky-blues, purples, and violets have now faded to buffs and greys, beautiful in themselves, but quite different from the bright hues that attracted the original purchaser. Often the precious harmony achieved by artists like Harunobu is destroyed when the more stable greens, yellows, and chocolate browns remain unimpaired while the other hues become dulled.

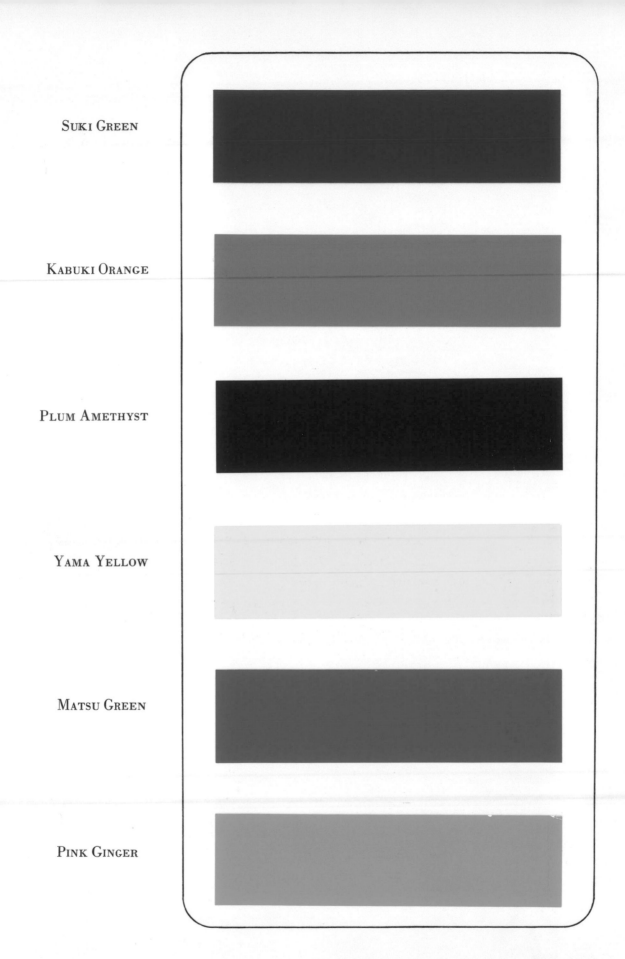

SUKI GREEN

KABUKI ORANGE

PLUM AMETHYST

YAMA YELLOW

MATSU GREEN

PINK GINGER

NOWHERE is color so effective an artistic instrument as in mediaeval illuminated manuscripts. In one masterpiece of Dutch miniature painting, *The Hours of Catherine of Cleves* (now in the collection of the Morgan Library in New York City), the stress of iridescence transmutes everyday artifacts into objects of luxury.

Undertaken as a wedding present for Catherine, who married Arnold, Duke of Guelders in 1430, the manuscript is a compendium of devotional texts that takes its name from one essential text, The Hours of the Virgin. It is called "Hours" or "Horae" in Latin because it is sub-divided into eight parts, one for each of the hours of the liturgical day.

Refinement and exactitude mark the forms and the color of *The Hours*. The degree of exactitude can perhaps best be comprehended when it is realized that some of the details, like jumping fish, measure one thirty-second of an inch. So jewel-like and precious are the painted colors that silver and gold, which are used in practically all the miniatures, never seem foreign but a part of the general delight in a luxurious palette of cherry-reds, white lemon yellows, mauves, brown golds, clear golds, and deep, medium, and light blues and greens.

Undoubtedly the most unusual aspect of *The Hours* are the trompe-l'oeil still-life borders. In one border, for example, there are open pods with golden peas symbolizing fertility. The illusion that the peas are real is heightened by the way in which the vines seem to pierce the vellum of the page. Another dramatically effective border is composed of eleven mussels open, with their inner tissues painted gold, their shells in blues and white blues.

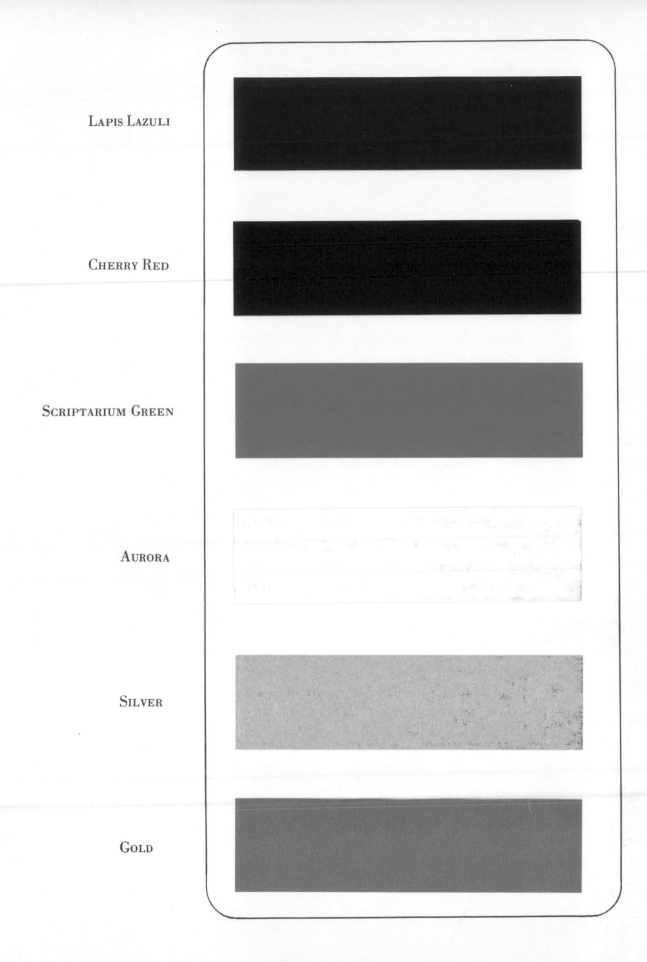

LAPIS LAZULI

CHERRY RED

SCRIPTARIUM GREEN

AURORA

SILVER

GOLD

COLORS FROM AFRICAN MASKS

MAN IN every age has had the desire to transcend himself, and in fulfilling this need the mask offers an ideal means. Behind African masking is the idea that the spirit represented by the mask temporarily takes possession of its wearer. As the chief appurtenances of ritual dances, African masks function in burial feasts, harvest festivals, initiation rites and on many other occasions to ensure tribal welfare. These complex and subtle social functions of African art are only beginning to be understood. But as aesthetic objects, masks in particular have been prized by non-African artists and connoisseurs since the beginning of the twentieth century.

In the use of color, masks show a greater richness than is seen elsewhere in African art. Alongside the monochrome masks, there are some which are violent and aggressive in color.

With the exception of certain tribes who favor bronze, wood is the basic material of African masks, but every conceivable trimming, including animal skins, metals, pearls, shells, is attached. The African almost always relies on black, white and red for decoration. These colors are easily accessible to him. Moreover, they evoke definite associations: white suggests the supernatural, danger, and death; black often symbolizes earth; and red implies energy and joy. Besides black and stark white, key African mask colors are a bluish-caste white, a deeply saturated red, turquoise green and a deep gray-blue.

Courtesy, Tribal Arts Gallery, New York

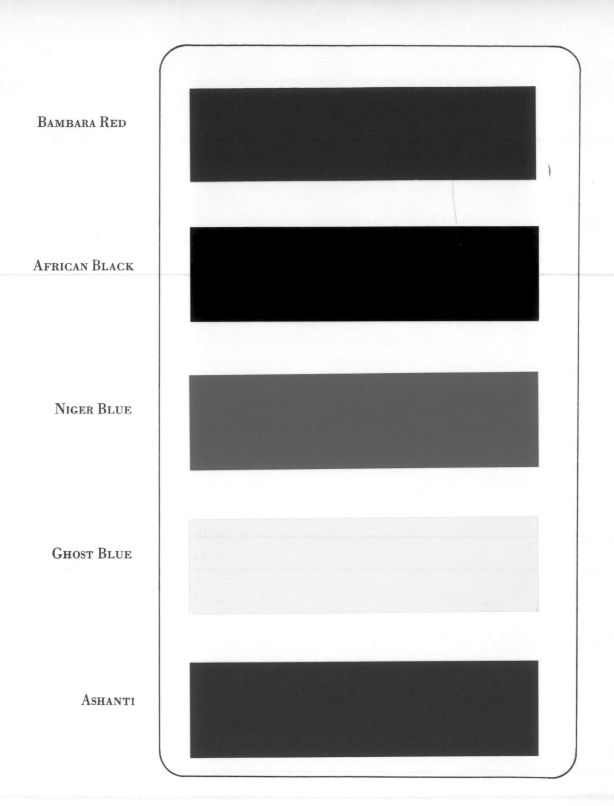

BAMBARA RED

AFRICAN BLACK

NIGER BLUE

GHOST BLUE

ASHANTI

COLORS FROM AFRICAN MASKS   27

COLONIAL AND FEDERAL AMERICAN COLORS

BECAUSE our pre-revolutionary tradition was so profoundly influenced by the British, the decorative style and palette of Colonial America (shown in the restored houses of Williamsburg) strongly reflected early Georgian taste. The Colonial American palette showed a similar English preference for green — light Georgian, deep Georgian, and Queen Anne Green. Generally, the reds, blues, yellows, tans, greys, and golds seen in Virginia, Charleston, and Philadelphia colonial homes are lighter than their early Georgian counterparts. Climate may have had something to do with this, for paler shades are usually preferred in sunny regions.

With the Revolution, America cut ties with England. During the Federal period a unique American palette emerged. Salem White was widely used, particularly for upper walls. Newport Yellow and Virginia Green are two historic examples of this nation's unique taste for tones of pale yellow-green. Also unique to this country are gold variations like Windsor Gold (a grey-gold), Charleston Green (a gold-green), and Perry Gold (a brown-gold). All these colors were usually applied to lower walls with white above. Cupboard Red is as American as apple pie. Regardless of the wall color, the corner cabinet revealed Cupboard Red.

CUPBOARD RED

CHARLESTON GREEN

PERRY GOLD

SALEM WHITE

VIRGINIA GREEN

NEWPORT YELLOW

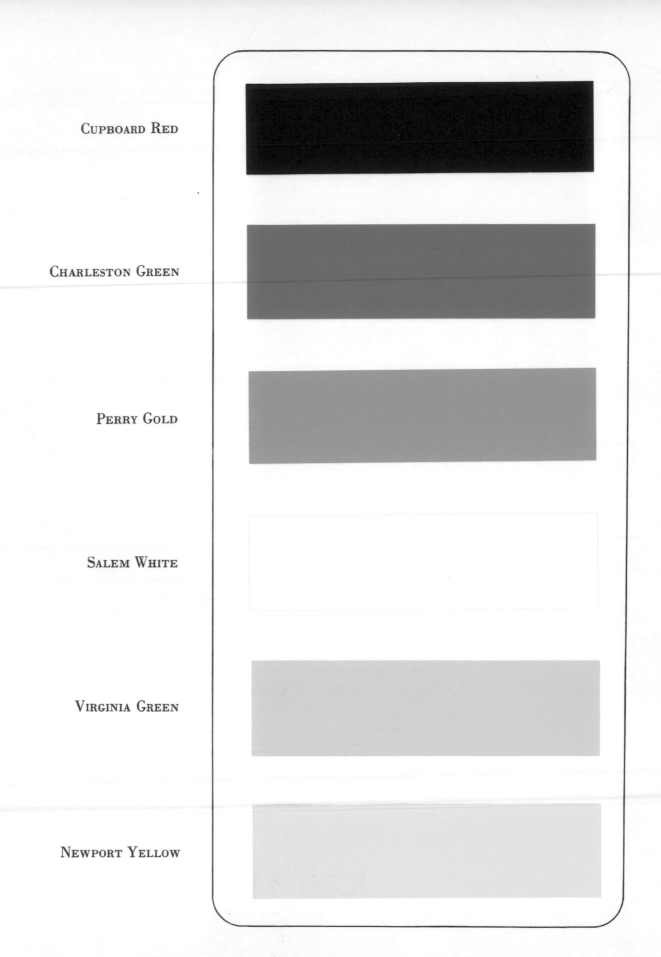

WILLIAMSBURG COLORS

FROM 1699 to 1780, Williamsburg was the capital of Virginia. Since 1693, it has been the site of the College of William and Mary. In colonial Williamsburg, the resident population never exceeded 2,000, but as the political and cultural center of Great Britain's largest and wealthiest continental colony, the little city was very important.

Today, Williamsburg offers the visitor the unique opportunity of seeing one of British North America's most historic colonial cities. In 1926, Rev. William A. R. Goodwin conceived of the idea of restoring the entire city. He interested John D. Rockefeller, Jr., who agreed to provide the funds, which ultimately totalled more than $62,000,000. Restoration work began in 1928. In the course of the work, 731 modern buildings were torn down, 81 existing buildings were restored, and 413 buildings were completely reconstructed on their original foundations.

For the accurate restoration of colonial Williamsburg, many problems had to be resolved by intensive architectural and historic research. Take, for example, the problem of ascertaining the original paint colors. Most colonial paints were imported from England in dry form to be ground and mixed with oil by their users. Only by painstakingly stripping away layer upon layer of paint and wallpaper, by allowing for oxidation, by searching for areas of paint that were covered by furniture or applied woodwork and by cross-checking these with colonial American and early Georgian examples have the original Williamsburg paint colors been duplicated.

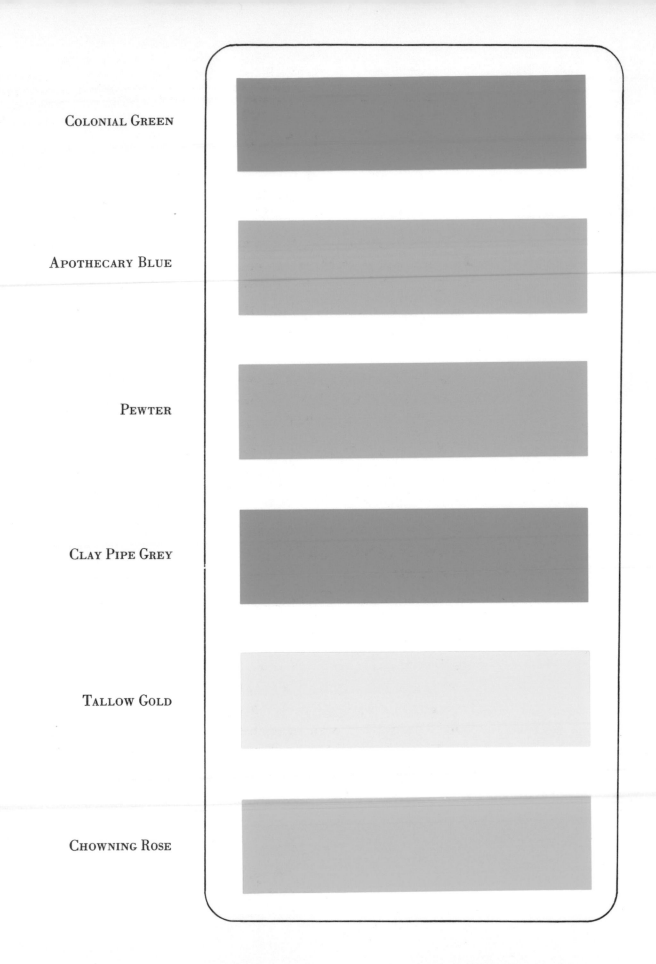

Colonial Green

Apothecary Blue

Pewter

Clay Pipe Grey

Tallow Gold

Chowning Rose

BATIK COLORS

WESTERN designers have been intrigued by the jungle opulence of batik design and colors ever since the Dutch traders first brought back samples of this marvelous cloth from Java in the seventeenth century.

"Batik" in Javanese means wax painting, and the art of batik is at least two thousand years old. Hot wax is traced onto a fabric so that when it is initially dyed the wax sections will remain uncolored in preparation for future dyeings. Although the word itself denotes this process, it has come to stand for a distinctive school of decorative fabrics.

Batik colors consist of the muted browns and golds and smokey blues of vegetable dyes. The colors most often used in Java are blue from indigo, yellow from the bark of mangosteen, and red from madder. Contrasting strongly with these muted colors are the swirling, kaleidoscopic batik designs.

Although originally Javanese batik workers were far more absorbed with the creation of intricate designs than with the use of color, European and American artisans, in developing their own versions of this ancient art, evolved a broad palette of vibrant hues. In the sixties, the charm and subtlety of the original palette returned to favor, both within the batik fabric design and in a myriad of other applications.

INDIGO

MANGOSTEEN

MADDER

SMOKEY BLUE

MUTED BROWN

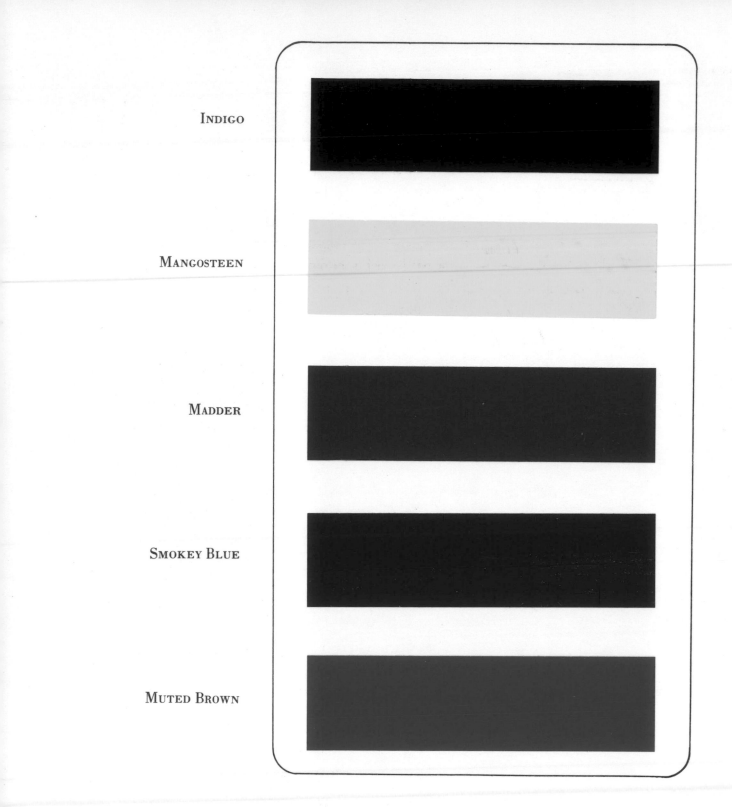

SCOTTISH TARTAN COLORS

IT IS difficult to describe the characteristic Scottish quality of the basic greens, blues and reds traditionally used by the clans for their tartan plaids. The hardy wools used and the inherent difficulties encountered in dyeing with primitive dye derivatives undoubtedly contributed much to the special flavor of the original tartan colors.

The name Tartan means a pattern or design (plaid) consisting of an arrangement of cross bars in varying colors and widths. The name, however, has become generic, designating a type of fabric or, more specifically, the complete Scottish Highland costume. Early Roman garments were also made of fabrics that we now term tartans, and archaeology indicates that tartan-type fabrics date back to the early days of civilization along the Nile. The name Tartan was originally given to this type of dress by the Spanish; the French derivation was Tiretaine.

The emphasis placed on color by the early Scots is indicated by the fact that a clan might use one combination of colors for its so-called Dress Tartan, another for hunting, and a third for battle. It is interesting to note that with three or four basic colors the originators of the Tartans managed to achieve an astonishing number of inspired visual effects.

Douglas Blue

Argyll Green

Macleod Yellow

Cunningham Red

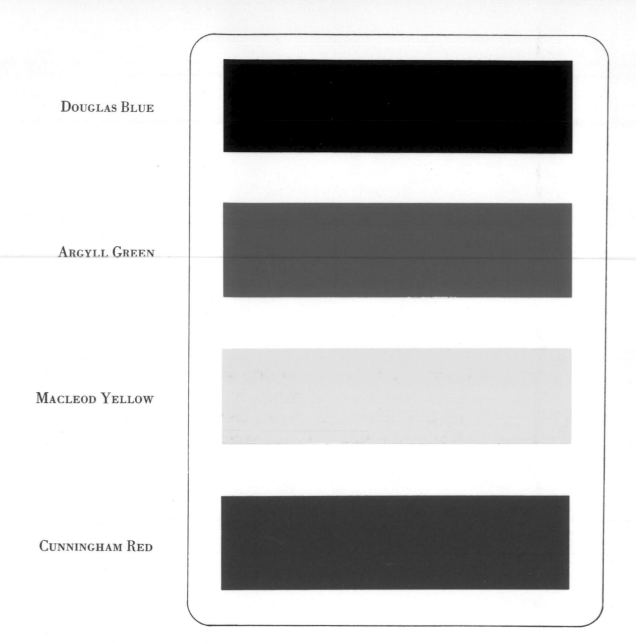

VICTORIAN COLORS

ALTHOUGH the decades of the Victorian era (1837-1901) may have marked a low ebb in the art of design, they did witness a defined taste in color and the discovery of the aniline dyes. In the home, the cornerstone of Victorian society, colors became darker, richer, and more pronounced, as Victoria's reign progressed and as interiors grew more elaborate and more crowded.

Color schemes in a typical Victorian interior connected the function of a room with its hues. Thus, dining rooms were decorated in warm, substantial hues, terms equally applicable to food; libraries were papered in grave, severe tones; halls and stairways in cool, impersonal tones; and parlors and drawing rooms in gay ones.

Rich, deep, yellowish greens, particularly Stuart Green and dark olive, and Pompeii Red were popular Victorian colors. A buff color was widely used and its drabness still haunts walls in Great Britain today. Tobacco brown and taupe were also favorite colors.

The decade of the "Gay Nineties" is known as the Mauve Decade. The color honors William Henry Perkins who discovered the first of the artificial or aniline dyes in 1856. The new brilliant purple-pinks, "magenta" and "solferino" (named after two battles in the Austro-Italian war of 1859) were by far the most popular shades of the aniline dyes. Other historic examples of these potent dyes are Victorian Blue, Victorian Green, and Victorian Orange.

PARLOR MAUVE

STUART GREEN

BARK OLIVE

SOLFERINO

LIBRARY TOBACCO

HALLWAY BUFF

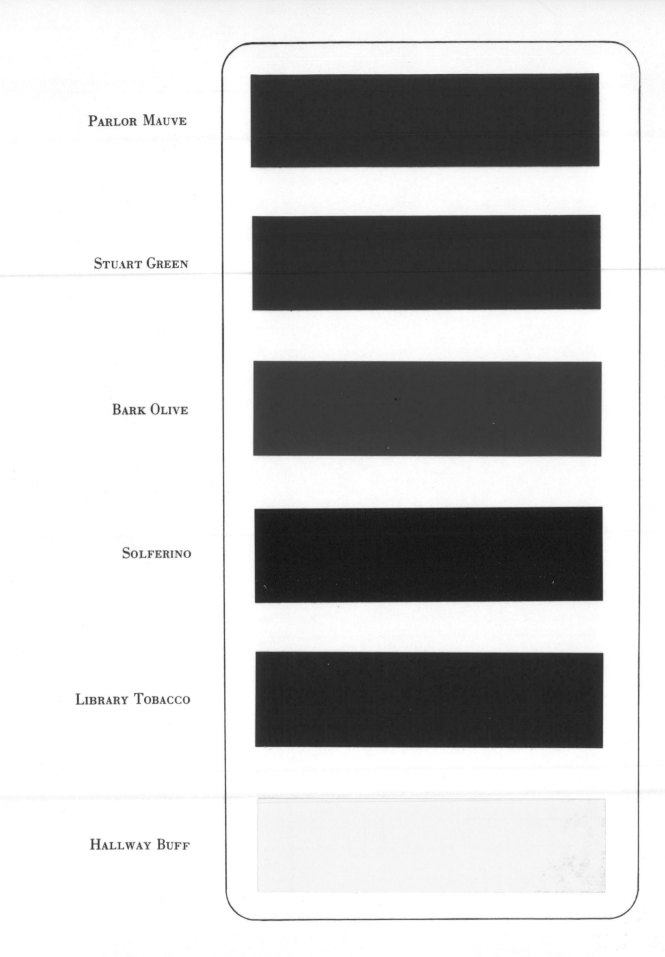

THE COLORS OF GREEK POTTERY

THERE is full awareness of the design which came from Ancient Greece, but knowledge of Greek color is negligible. This is because the forms we now see have lost all their color. Originally the Greek statues were painted, but the paint has disappeared with time. The Greeks also made wall paintings which they considered the highest form of artistic expression, ranking even above their marvelous architecture and sculpture. But none of these murals have survived.

Today Greek pots are our only surviving source of an Ancient Greek color palette. The colors of extant Greek pottery are the muted rusts and blacks of the black-figure style and the red-figure style made popular by Athenian craftsmen from the end of the seventh century B.C. to the beginning of the fourth century B.C.

The black-figure style came to maturity in the sixth century when the ornamental flora and fauna receded to allow the central figure to dominate. These figures were drawn in black silhouette and contrasted strongly with the natural red of the attic clay. Red ochre was often mixed into the clay to heighten its original color. About 520 B.C. the introduction of the red-figure style reversed the process. The main figures were reserved in red clay while the background was painted black.

About 400 B.C. tempera color—reds, yellows, blues, purples, greens, mauves, and pinks— was applied after the pottery had been fired, and thus today can be seen only in severely faded examples. What is still to be seen of this later vase painting style are the subtle bone white to sand hues of the backgrounds.

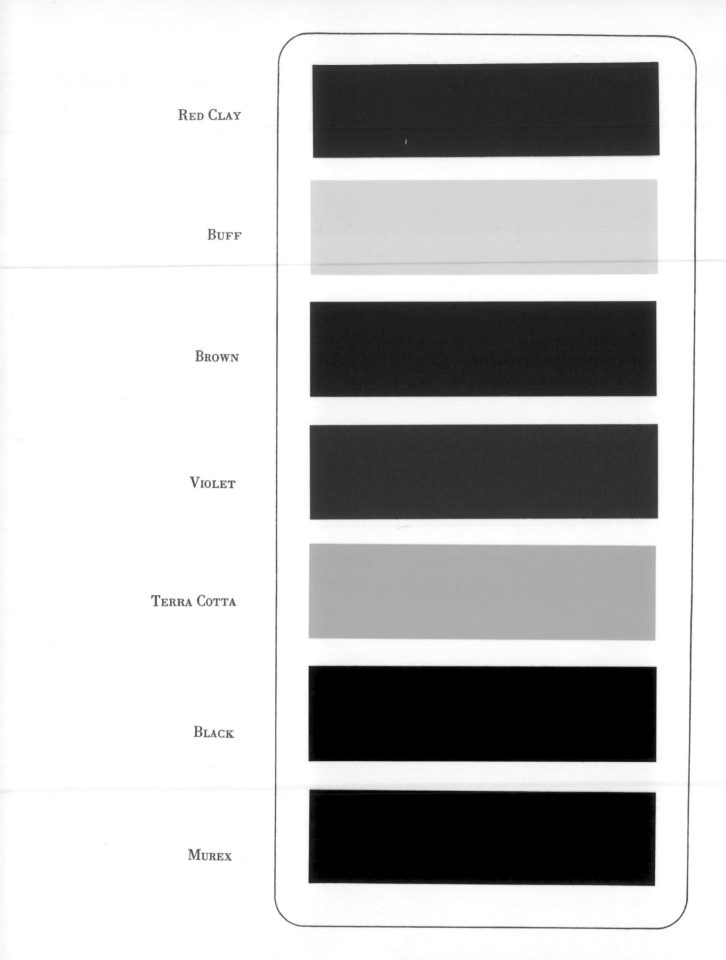

RED CLAY

BUFF

BROWN

VIOLET

TERRA COTTA

BLACK

MUREX

INDIAN TEXTILE COLORS

INDIA'S art is inseparable from her religion. To understand the extraordinary intensity of color found in Indian Textiles, one must view them within their religious context.

India's centuries-old Hindu caste system has nurtured generations upon generations of specialized craftsmen, superbly skilled in block printing, resist dyeing, tie-dyeing and mordant dyeing. Hinduism also accounts for a rich symbolism, which gives meaning to every facet of life, including color. Practically all of India's many deities have a special color. Red is the color of Brahma, the creator; white of Shiva, the destroyer; and blue of Krishna, the preserver. When worn by the Indians, these colors become a projection of the gods enshrined in their temples. Deep gold yellow and glowing vermilion are ceremonial colors. Traditionally, brides wear ivory tones.

The incredibly hot colors of Indian textiles take into account the catalytic power of the sun. In India, colors mature and fade to softer hues in response to the sun. Also taken into account was the effect of color against dark-toned skins. From earliest times India's dyemakers used al root or lac for reds; indigo for blues; pomegranate rinds for greens; tumeric for yellows; and iron particles and vinegar for blacks. The colors chosen are those most frequently used in Indian fabrics today. All are characteristically hot and reflect a sun-bleached luminosity.

Hot Magenta

Kashmir Green

Bengal Orange

Ajanta Gold

Hot Turquoise

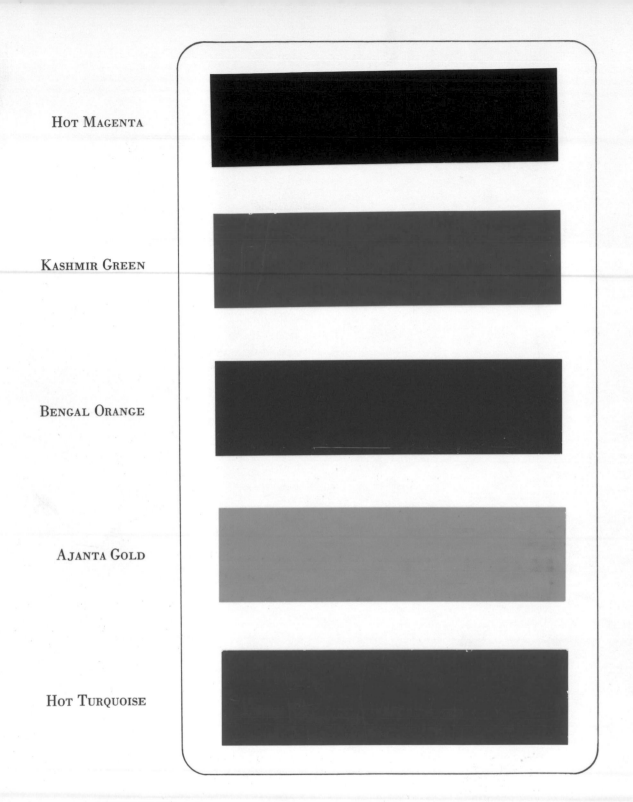

PERSIAN CARPET COLORS

THE HISTORY of Persian carpets is closely connected with the ruling house of the Safavid Dynasty, founded by Ismail I in 1499. Ismail I was succeeded by Shah Tahmasp and Shah Abbas the Great in the sixteenth and early seventeenth centuries, and it was the reigns of these two great rulers that witnessed the golden age of the Persian carpet. Under Shah Tahmasp, the Turkish abstract patterns that had dominated rug design until the end of the fifteenth century were replaced by a medallion style, which was created not by the weavers but rather by the painters and illuminators of the court school. Later, under Shah Abbas the Great, the so-called vase carpet, of progressive floral design which springs from a vase, and the tree carpet and garden carpet were first made.

Persian carpets owe their incredible beauty to their arabesque designs of the highest realism and complexity on the one hand and to the secret skills of the dyer on the other. In the old days each dyer was responsible for just one dye. To be a dyer of blue or red carried the highest status in a village. Madder, sheep's blood, grapes, kermes insect, vine leaves, berries, mulberry leaves, ivy, myrtle — all things that grew within the kin of the dyer were tried to their utmost as possible color-makers and color-changers.

Chosen for our palette of Persian carpet colors is padshah blue, dark, deep, and yet translucent. This blue was an essential color in all high class Persian carpets. Also chosen is Persian Old Rose, Islam red, ivory, and Persian turquoise.

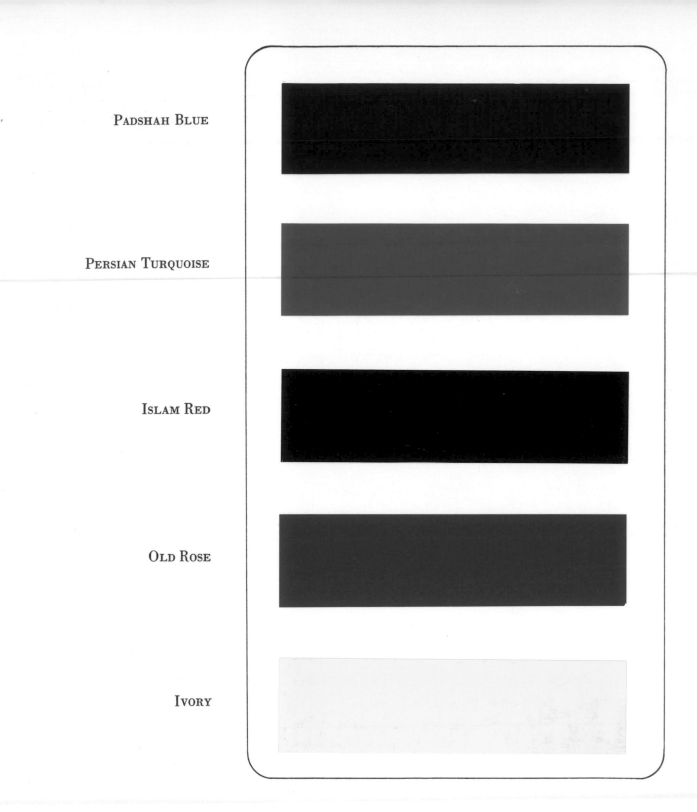

PADSHAH BLUE

PERSIAN TURQUOISE

ISLAM RED

OLD ROSE

IVORY

COPTIC TEXTILE COLORS

THE art of Christian Egypt in the period between the fourth and ninth centuries is called Coptic (from an Arabic corruption, *kipt*, of the Greek word for Egypt, *Aigyptios*). Coptic art flourished in monastic centers up the Nile, away from the sophisticated, Hellenized Alexandria. Various aesthetic strains — those of Ancient Egypt, of Greece, of Rome, and of the Near East — merged to form the essentially decorative and provincial style of the Copts. The unmistakable individuality of Coptic art comes across whether it be the crudely conventionalized, frontal depiction of figures or the equally sharply outlined and boldly flat rendering of foliage in geometric patterns.

Undoubtedly, fresco painting and textiles were the outstanding achievements of the Copts. Thanks to the great preservative powers of the dry climate of Egypt, the original colors can be seen today in remnants of covers, wall hangings, and tunics. Most of these fabrics are linen with tapestry woven ornament in wool.

Bold colors reinforce the powerful folk designs of Coptic textiles. In place of modelling, we find a sharp contrast of deeply saturated colors. A very deep purple was used most extensively. Yet, the pervading tonality is brown, for the Copts seem to have delighted in the decorative effect achieved by opposing one brown against another. The scale of browns ranges from an orange-brown to a very deep, almost black, brown.

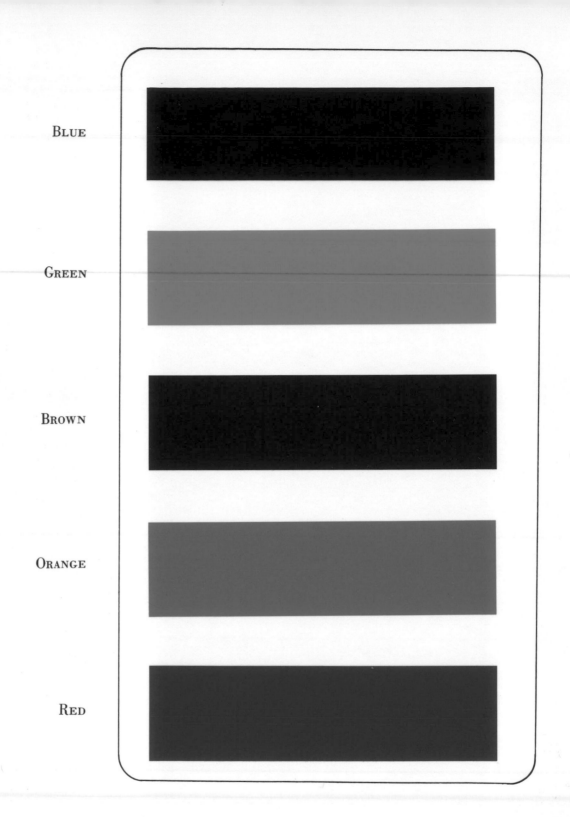

BLUE

GREEN

BROWN

ORANGE

RED

COLORS OF THE AMERICAN INDIANS
OF THE SOUTHWEST

LIKE their ancestors, the American Indians of the Southwest still draw upon their environment to create a lasting art. The rich colors of the Arizona and New Mexico deserts seem to infuse their geometrically designed fabrics with a vitality that transports their craftsmanship into the realm of art.

The color palette employed by the Southwest Indians is limited. In the finest Navajo blankets, one seldom finds more than five colors, including black and white. The colors employed are strong and dignified primaries — grass green, a deep red, a dark blue, and a lemon yellow. A good example of Navajo textile artistry is woven in what is commonly called the "chief's blanket" design. Red, blue, black, and undyed wool are the colors of the geometric pattern, which remains the same even when the blanket is folded in quarters.

Like the Navajo, the Hopi artisan also employs few colors, usually blue, green, white, black, and a touch of red. Very ancient in type and strikingly beautiful are the Hopi ceremonial shawls. The ground is white, but across the top and bottom run bold bands of green and black. The lower borders usually contain five diamond-shaped medallions in bright greens and reds while black triangles, symbols of rain clouds, rise onto the sand-white field of cloth above.

In their use of dignified and strong colors, with a very limited range, the Indians of the American Southwest are a source of present-day inspiration.

GRASS GREEN

DARK RED

DARK BLUE

PRAIRIE YELLOW

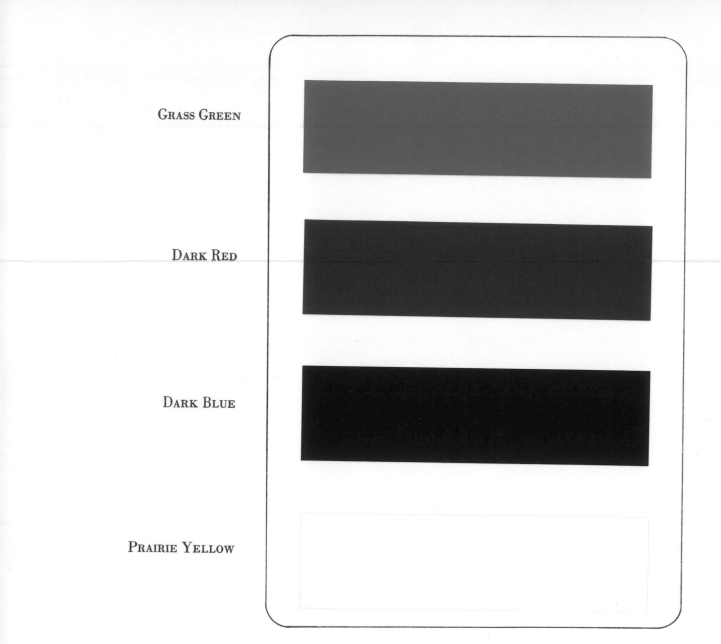

GOBELIN TAPESTRY COLORS

IN THE 15th century, a family of dyers by the name of Gobelin established a tapestry workshop on the outskirts of Paris. This factory, purchased by finance minister Colbert in 1662 to provide facilities for two Flemish weavers whom he had brought over to establish looms in Paris, has given its name to the famous tapestries.

At the outset, the factory was intended as a royal upholstery works. Colbert soon recruited Charles Le Brun as its director. The change in management saw a corresponding shift in production. Tapestries became its primary and, indeed, exclusive, concern. Soon the factory was weaving the huge figure work for which Gobelin tapestries became world famous.

From the multitude of colors used in Gobelin Tapestries we have selected a palette of clear, warm shades which typify some of the great works of art produced here during the high-point of Gobelin fame in the mid-18th century

DEEP BROWN

CARNATION

PALE BROWN

GOBELIN GREY

BLUE

RED

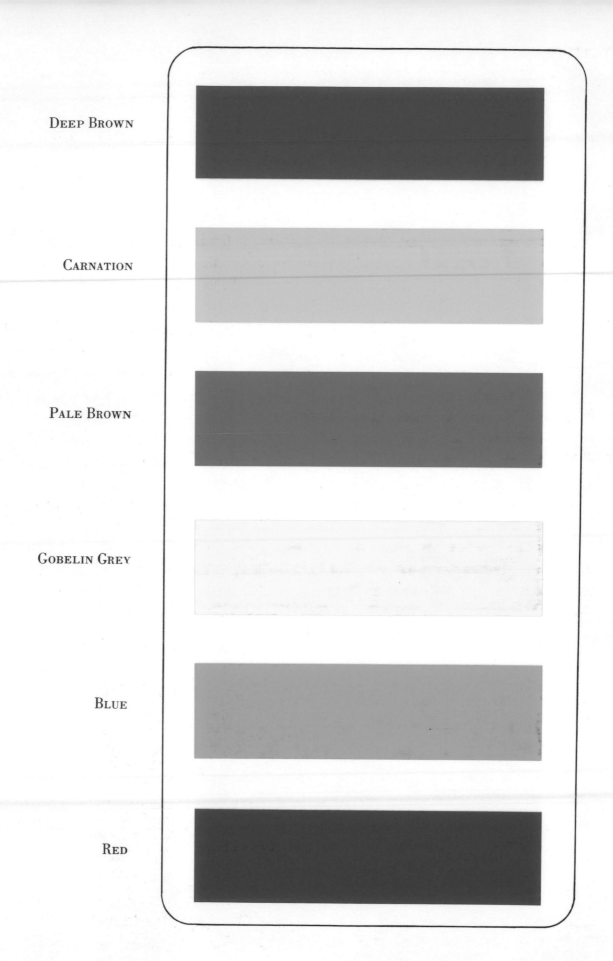

AUBUSSON TAPESTRY COLORS

FOR THE decorator, the designs and colors of the Aubusson Tapestries provide an endless source of inspiration. Their superb balance and precision are of illimitable use.

The Aubusson tapestry factory, founded toward the end of the 13th century and staffed by immigrant weavers from Flanders, reached the height of its creative activity toward the middle of the 18th century. During this period of some fifty years, there appeared outstanding tapestries woven after the designs of Jean Baptiste Oudry and François Boucher.

Oudry's famous Hunt scenes with their vitality and clear colors no less than the whimsey and elegance of Boucher's classic designs inspired the creation of thousands of new dyes. The result was that these tapestries became, indeed, paintings in wool or silk.

Chinese and Medallion designs were favored by the less well-known artists among them Fragonard, Huet and Lancret. Unlike the elaborate creations of Boucher and Oudry, these tapestries tended toward more sombre hues and were produced in great quantity.

AUBUSSON GREEN

BOUCHER BLUE

INCARNADINE

AUBUSSON RED

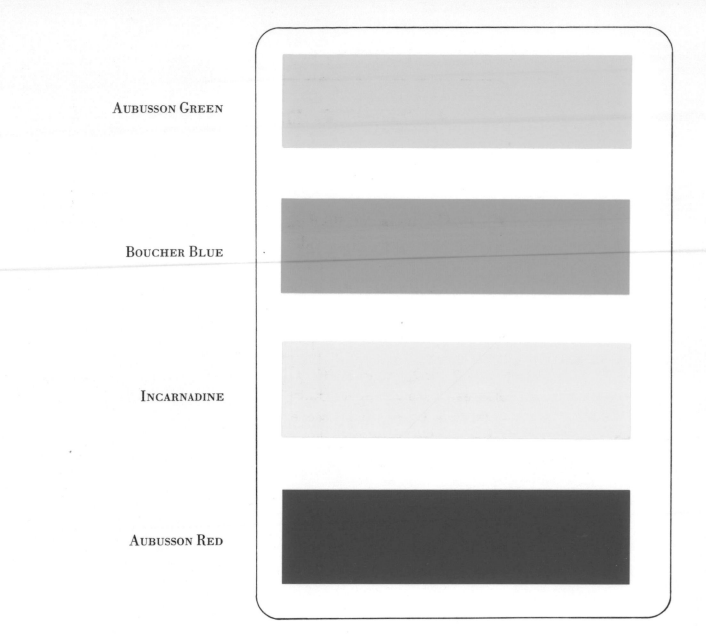

EMPIRE COLORS

THE DEEP and intense luminosity of Empire colors reflect the power and optimism of France's First and Second Empires with which they are associated. In both mood and aesthetics the nation shifted away from the harsh asceticism of the Revolution. Richly and deeply colored, decorative motifs were taken directly from Greece, Rome and Egypt, lands made familiar to the French by Napoleon's conquests.

Empire Green, a vivid color which Napoleon favored (along with white and gold) was originally used for the draperies and furniture of the State Rooms. Probably Empire Green was derived from Chinese Cucumber ware which was popular during the First Empire. Its exact tint was fixed by the regulations of state dyers.

The colors which complemented Empire Green (in an Empire palette to Napoleon's liking) were clear lemon yellow, a deep pearl grey, a rosy red, a deep ruby, azure blue and amethyst.

Napoleon did not have his way in the choice of colors all the time, however. He was wed to an Empress, Josephine. She brought to the deep Empire palette the genteel taste of her royal predecessors for muted colors. Hence, gray-blue and pale ivory also are a part of the Empire palette.

EMPIRE GREEN

PEARL GREY

AMETHYST

EMPIRE RUBY

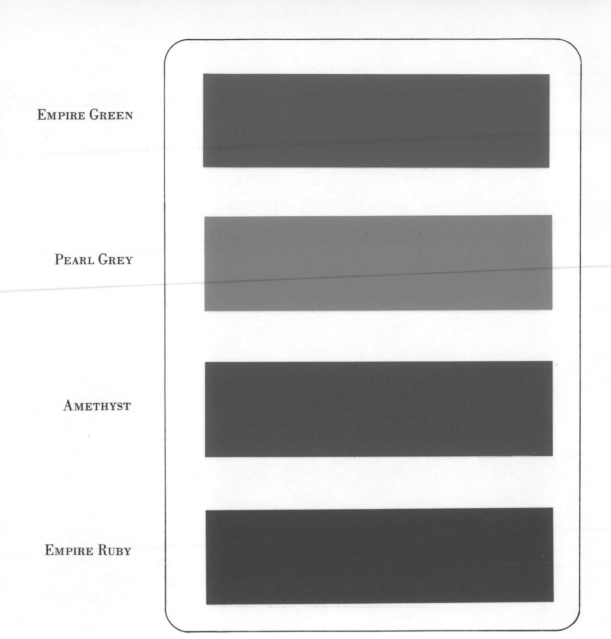

WEDGWOOD COLORS

ENGLAND'S Josiah Wedgwood founded a family of potters and a palette of colors that have made his name a household word.

Born in 1730, Wedgwood made innovations in his Staffordshire factory that established an international market surviving to this day. Influenced profoundly by the eighteenth-century classical revival, Wedgwood's ideas found expression not only in his well-known pots but in furniture and architectural insets as well.

The Wedgwood family of colors has many famous offspring. So widespread was the fame of Wedgwood pottery that its most popular shade was given the character of a generic term and is now universally known as "Wedgwood Blue." However, there was far more than one shade in the Wedgwood range. At least three Wedgwood blues were used — pale, medium, and deep. In addition, there was a famous lilac, a cane yellow and a group of Jasper (quartz) colors which included a brick red with a pinkish cast, a pale avocado green, and a warm bark brown.

The Wedgwood color palette is a very subtle one with almost unlimited possibilities of application. Wedgwood pieces rarely employ but a single hue plus white. Modern taste, however, enjoys numerous permutations and combinations amongst the original palette.

JOSIAH WEDGWOOD
Feb 2 *or* 2nd Feby 1805

DEEP WEDGWOOD BLUE

LILAC

PALE WEDGWOOD BLUE

MEDIUM WEDGWOOD BLUE

JASPER RED

JASPER GREEN

JASPER BROWN

JASPER CANE YELLOW

WEDGWOOD COLORS

THE ADAM GREENS

THE FAMOUS Adam brothers, particularly Robert Adams, revolutionized the decorative arts in England in the late 18th century. Late Georgian really means the Adam brothers.

Scottish by birth and an architect by training, Robert Adam travelled extensively in Italy in the 1750's and returned to England to base his style on the Greco-Roman ruins. His light and delicate, classically inspired style can still be seen in England's fine late 18th century mansions.

Color, in all its modulations and applications played an important part in the Adam school of design; and of all the colors, green — in the subtle gradations shown here — was by far the most favored.

Pastel tints, very compatible with classical forms, are most frequently associated with Robert Adam's style. Adam colors, however, include colors of depth — strong blues and green, sumptuous reds and lively lilacs and apricots — as well as opal tints. Though based upon the classical palette (and especially the frescoes at Pompeii), the Adam colors tend generally to be slightly cooler, more elegant, "prettier" in the best sense of the word than are the prototypes.

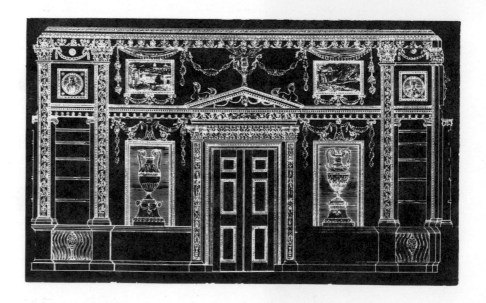

MEDIUM GREEN

PALE ADAM GREEN

DEEP GREEN

POMPEII RED

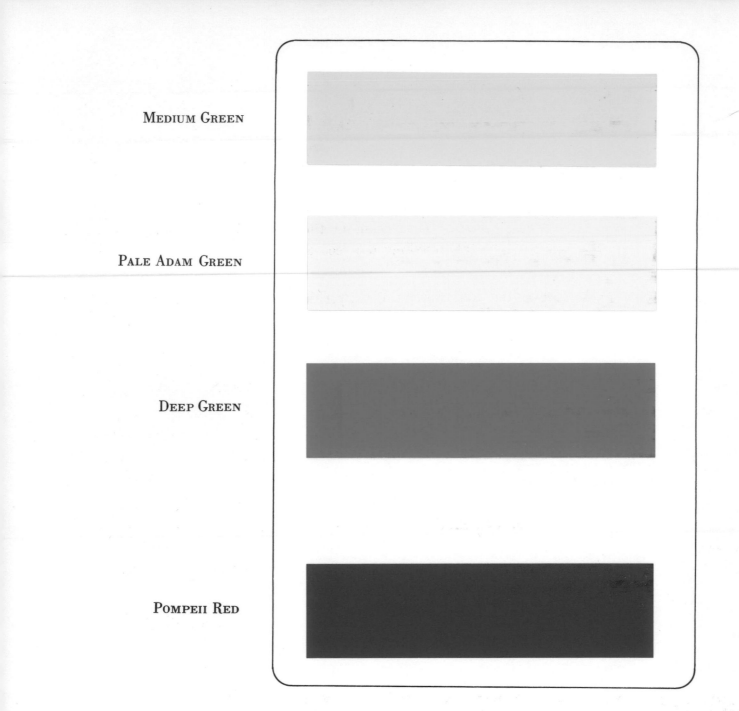

GIOTTO'S PALETTE

IN THE history of art, Giotto stands out as the first of the great Italian masters of the Renaissance. Giotto, claimed the Renaissance writer Boccaccio, resuscitated painting after it has been "in the grave." Unquestionably, the interest of his contemporaries rested on Giotto's realism, for Giotto's art marks a return to the naturalistic traditions of Antiquity.

In their colors, Giotto's frescoes mark a decided move away from the Byzantine tradition toward a lighter and more varied palette. To achieve tactile values, Giotto used light color schemes so that he could accentuate contrasts and thus build volumes. Giotto's palette is basically composed of warm, dense, yet clear colors which seem to anticipate and appropriate the quality of chiaroscuro (the modelling in the light and shade of later Renaissance painters).

In 1304 Giotto began his most important commission, the completely frescoed interior of the Arena Chapel in Padua. The work was financed by Enrico Scrovegni to atone for the misdeeds of his father who was so avaricious that Dante sets him in the seventh circle of Hell. Soft lavenders, mauves, grey blues, grey greens, deep greens, and the unique flesh tone of beige with the palest tint of pink are dominant in the Paduan cycle. These warm and limpid colors accentuate the humanity of the events depicting Christ's birth and life.

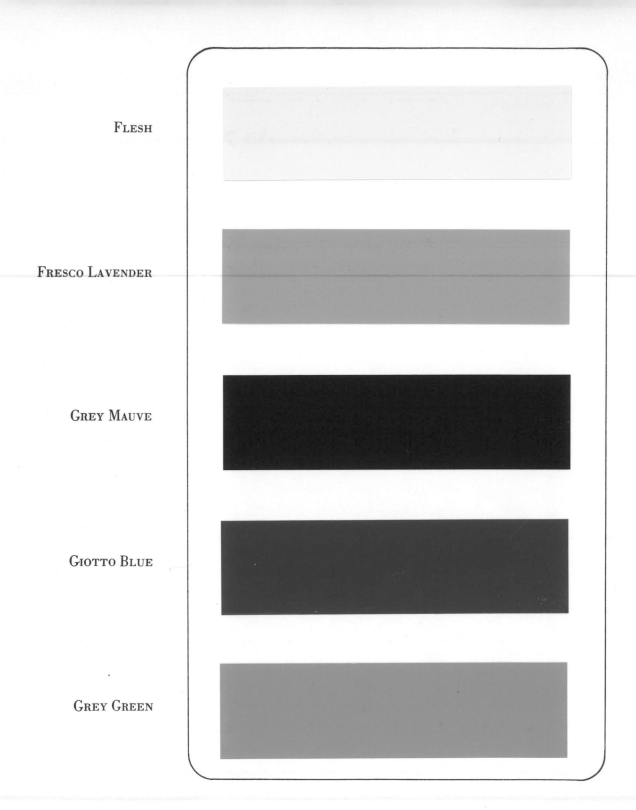

FLESH

FRESCO LAVENDER

GREY MAUVE

GIOTTO BLUE

GREY GREEN

PIERO DELLA FRANCESCA'S PALETTE

MASTER of serene colors, adept in geometry and mathematics, and the creator of contemplative, monumental forms, Piero della Francesca stands out, between Masaccio and Leonardo, as one of the greatest painters of the Italian Renaissance. Of all the Renaissance painters, Piero is the most appealing to the twentieth century colorist, for his colors come from a legendary world built both on reality and abstraction.

Piero was emphatically not one of those painters who, in Leonardo's phrase, "live by the beauty of blue and gold." Somberness and frugality mark Piero's palette. His colors are fundamentally the somber tones of the Tuscan vineyards, grey olives, brown earth, purple grapes, green vineleaves, the lavender of faded blue garments of peasants, and the white of oxen. To enliven this grave harmony, Piero used, but sparingly, the warm colors of pink and subdued red. His two colors of dignity, reserved for rare occasions, were a very deep pomegranate red, on the verge of porphyry, and a Mandarin blue.

Piero's major work was a series of frescoes narrating the story of the True Cross and done for the Church of San Francesco in Arezzo in the mid-fifteenth century. Chosen for our palette are four colors from the Arezzo frescoes: pomegranate red, a bone flesh tone with the barest tint of pink, a grape purple, and a deep grey olive. These are outstanding examples of Piero's color abstractions from the Tuscan scene.

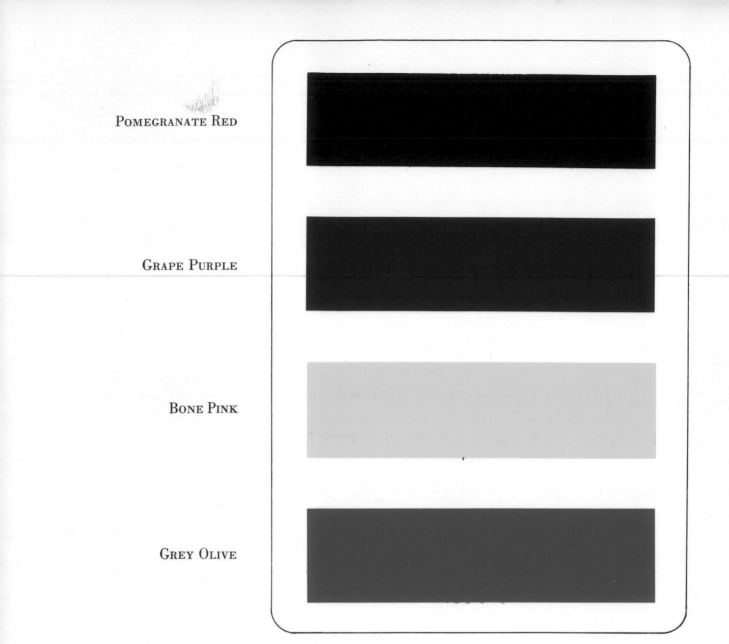

POMEGRANATE RED

GRAPE PURPLE

BONE PINK

GREY OLIVE

EL GRECO'S PALETTE

EL GRECO's art represents a clash of cultures — his Byzantine-Cretan heritage, the Italian Renaissance and Mannerist environments in which he was thoroughly grounded, and the religious temper of Spanish Toledo which he absorbed. His palette is unique, for his canvases literally glow with phosphorescent, hallucinagenic colors.

In Spain where the landscape is often monochrome, El Greco's palette reduced itself to five colors — ivory, vermilion, yellow ocher, ultramarine, and rose madder — and mixtures thereof. In addition he used pure black and white. Through color juxtapositions of acid brillance — such as green set off with chartreuse and red-orange against green — he produced chromatic effects of an unparalleled eerie and spectral nature. Along with such dazzling color contrasts, El Greco used pure leaden white to accentuate his attenuated forms. Through these chromatic devices his forms seem to glow inwardly and to enter a metaphysical realm.

For the twentieth century colorist, El Greco provides a lesson in the modulations of a limited number of hues for expressionistic purposes. His painting, *El Espolio*, 1579 (The Disrobing of Christ), in the Toledo Cathedral is a perfect example of how color can take on an expressive independence and can become in effect the narrator of a religious drama. In this work the burning ruby of Christ's robe consumes the cool tonalities that gravitate around its flame — the greys, the icy ochers, blues, and violets. Key colors in El Greco's palette are icy white blue, chalk grey, flaming ruby, and his famous acid chartreuse.

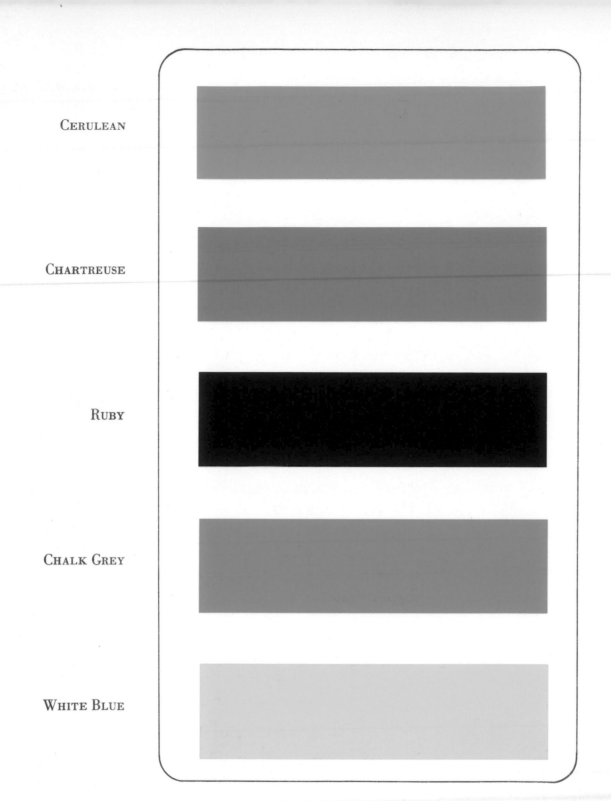

CERULEAN

CHARTREUSE

RUBY

CHALK GREY

WHITE BLUE

RUBENS'S BAROQUE PALETTE

IF THE life of Sir Peter Paul Rubens (1577-1640) could be summed up in one word, that word would be "energy." His art, characterized by vitality and passion, is the quintessence of the grandiose Baroque style. In the choice of subject matter, Rubens showed a predilection for women of large proportions, dazzling skin and golden hair, all of which called into play a sumptuous palette.

Rubens started painting in primaries, but under the aristocratic patronage of the grand heads of European states — indeed his collected portraits comprises a virtual "Who's Who" in seventeenth century Europe — he developed a sumptuous palette of rich purples and golds offset by the tertiaries of lavenders and peaches.

Rubens probably understood better than any other painter in history how to achieve the extraordinary nuances of red, blue, white, and yellow that make up the color of flesh. Chosen for our palette are one of his famous peach flesh tones, a gaudy gold, and a rich lavender. These colors are taken from his most important commissioned work, a series of paintings depicting the life of Marie de Medici, widow of Frances' King Henry IV. Marie de Medici ordered the paintings in 1621 for the Luxemburg Palace, the extravagant residence she was then building in Paris. The elaborately contrived allegory of the pictures intertwines the Queen's life with Greek mythology. Neptune helps to speed her sea voyage to France; Jupiter and Juno attend her marriage. The contrast of the nude gods of Olympus and the elegantly robed French monarchs allowed Rubens' rich baroque palette to glow in full force.

PEACH

GOLD

DAMSON

ROUGE

THE PALETTE OF VELASQUEZ

VELASQUEZ is no colorist in the eyes of those who seek sensational effects of hue, or who see little difference between black, Van Dyke Brown or Prussian blue. Vivid colors only rarely appear in the paintings of the seventeenth-century Spanish artist. The palette of Velasquez, dominated by the cool effect of silvery light, is that of a colorist who picks out the chromatic nuances of light upon a motif whose chief local hues are deliberately restricted, carefully understated.

Born in 1599, Velasquez became court painter at the age of twenty-four. Almost his entire life was spent at the Spanish court in Madrid. His portraits chronicle the life of Philip IV, who succeeded to the throne at 16, and the lives of his brothers and his children. In these portraits, Velasquez's palette of a few sober colors received animation from two recurring techniques. First, he usually steeped his subjects in convergent light to achieve glowing color effects. Secondly, he invariably set off a large somberly colored area like brown or black with rich notes of shimmering colors. In his portraits, silks have one sheen, velvets another, and the faces and hands of his subjects animate the low pitch of his unified color key.

Rosy carmine, a deep carmine, a silvery grey, a blue-white and a brown are the colors chosen to represent the Velasquez palette. All these colors come from the wonderful effects Velasquez achieved in dealing with the elaborate embroidery and glossy silks in *Las Meninas*, a painting done in 1656. The central figure is the Infanta Margarita Maria, and from her emanates a silvery light that illuminates the vivid notes of carmine.

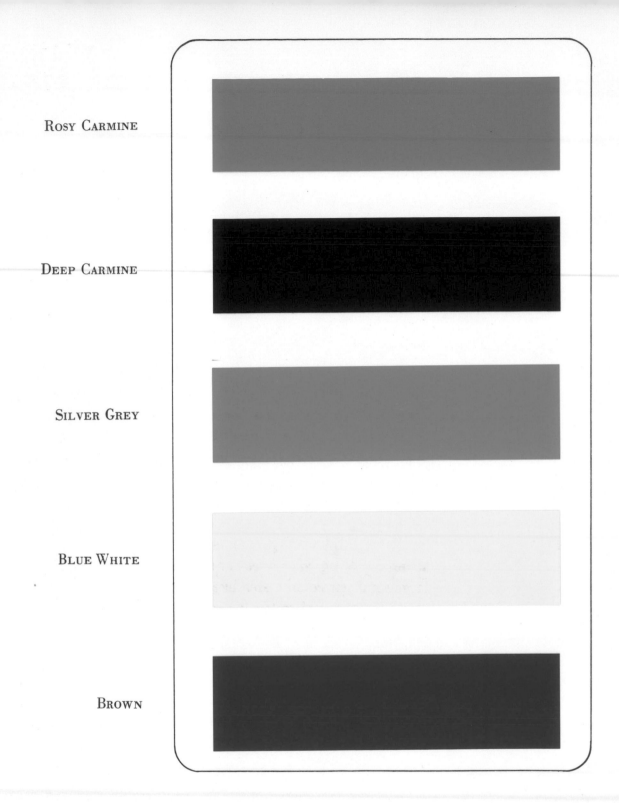

ROSY CARMINE

DEEP CARMINE

SILVER GREY

BLUE WHITE

BROWN

VERMEER'S PALETTE

JAN VERMEER, a near-contemporary of Rembrandt, and like him one of the greatest Dutch painters, offers a virtuoso palette of painted light. Vermeer based his color harmonies on the blue, grey, and pale yellow of a window facing north, and was the first to show the nuances of color in both shadow and daylight.

Streaming daylight, usually illuminating a young woman in a domestic seventeenth-century Dutch setting, is the recurring theme in Vermeer's art. Reflecting the contemplative mood of his genre interiors, Vermeer's palette is basically cool like daylight itself. The colors that regularly appear are ultramarine blue, lemon yellow, pearly grey, white, and a mixture of blue and brown that appears as a rich velvet near-black.

For Vermeer, and the other Old Masters, preparation of paints was a most difficult and time-consuming task, for commercially prepared paints only became available in the latter part of the nineteenth century. Easiest to procure and most used were brown and yellow earth colors. Yellow, from the deeply saturated hue of an illuminated woman's golden bodice to the palest reflection on the wall, played a key role in Vermeer's palette. Valuable colors like ultramarine blue and carmine were prepared in small quantities and preserved in pig's bladders from which they were squeezed when needed. Both ultramarine blue and carmine were used by Vermeer for dramatic effects.

Grinding his own colors (the finer the grains the lighter the color) allowed Vermeer to add something quite personal to his colors. Glazing (the glaze is the thin, semi-transparent layer of paint over a dried layer of paint) also allowed him endless possibilities in shading. Chosen from Vermeer's palette are two daylight yellows and two shades of daylight-illuminated ultramarine blue.

North Light Yellow

Dutch Yellow

Dutch Blue

North Light Blue

ITALIAN MANNERIST COLORS

For a long time the overpoweringly strident dissonances of Mannerist coloring were considered to be gross lapses of taste. Today, the Mannerists' researches into strange chromatic harmonies of cold and harsh hues — bright pinks, intense blues, raw greens, metallic yellows as well as a range of extremely pallid tones — are being considered as an excellent source of daring color schemes.

Mannerism can be characterized by its preoccupation with a *maniera,* or a style based less upon nature than upon art itself. Italian painters of the mid-sixteenth century shared, not one *maniera,* but a host of stylistic features which included an extreme clarity of contours, lustrous and elongated forms, strange perspective, and super-elegant gestures. Harsh colors made up the Mannerist palette.

The Mannerists were bold experimenters in color schemes. Jacopo da Pontormo's *Visitation* plays upon the close variations of acid greens contrasted with an equally fine range of pallid pinks and yellows. In Agnolo Bronzino's *Venus, Cupid, Time, and Folly,* there is a precious, albeit somewhat difficult to appreciate, beauty emanating from the combination of porcelain white flesh tones with intense blues and pinks, offset by touches of acid green and day-glow orange.

Chosen to represent the Mannerist palette are an acid green, a pallid pink, a vibrant blue, an abrasive day-glow orange, a very pale yellow, and a porcelain flesh tone.

ACID GREEN

PINK

VIBRANT BLUE

ORANGE

MANNERIST YELLOW

PORCELAIN

TURNER'S PALETTE

IN THE history of color expression the English romantic painter, Joseph Mallord William Turner, stands out. His vivid color effects anticipated Impressionism and much of abstract art.

Born in London in 1775, Turner studied at the Royal Academy as a young man. With the turn of the century his art became progressively more luminous and visionary. After his visit to Venice in 1819, light, or rather the colors of light, became the objective of his paintings and their true subject. The very names of his paintings — "Light and Color: Goethe's Theory" or "Sun Rising Through Vapor" attest to his interest in color and light.

According to contemporary accounts, Turner worked in a great hurry. (Too impatient to be a good technician, many of his paintings quickly deteriorated.) He worked with brush, knife, fingers, lumps of opaque paint, transparent glazes and varnishes. Working alternately with watercolor and oil, by the end of his life Turner handled oil as if it were watercolor.

In Turner's late paintings his palette plays on a sequence running from a tint or pastel to a grayish tone. In other words, light colors were pure, and deeper colors were neutralized or grayed. The over-all quality was grayish, and it created a field upon which his pure tints and pastels shone radiantly. Key colors in Turner's palette were white, a luminous yellow, and pure and muted variations of pink, orange, green, and blue, plus medium and deep greys.

Yellow

Pink

White

Green

Deep Grey

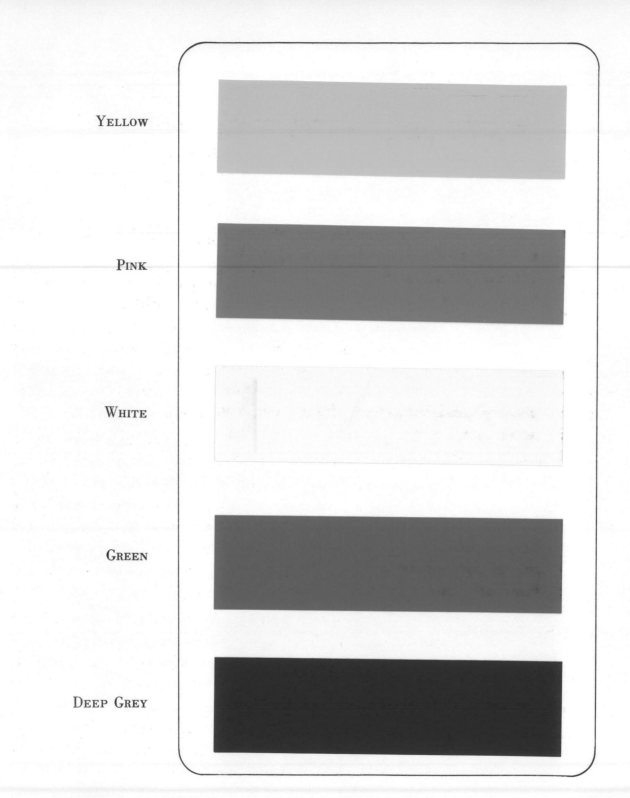

THE ROMANTIC PALETTE OF DELACROIX

THE leader of the nineteenth century French Romantic painting, called "the greatest palette of France" by Cezanne, Eugene Delacroix is unquestionably important in the history of color. Delacroix anticipated the Impressionists in his use of juxtaposed pure pigments. Quite frequently these juxtapositions place side by side hues from exact opposite positions of the color wheel to effect maximum brilliance. In his *Journal,* which is filled with penetrating references to color, he became one of the few great artists to give literary expression to his ideas.

In 1832 Delacroix spent four months travelling in North Africa as the artist attached to a special French mission to the Sultan of Morocco. His exposure to "the devil's sun" extended and intensified his palette and led him to experiment with more sparkling light effects. His Moroccan notebooks of drawings and watercolor sketches were to provide him with color material for the rest of his life. It is in these notebooks that his romantic palette, a veritable pictorial feast, emerged.

The Delacroix palette is striking for its dramatic use of emerald greens offset by lime yellows, pale blues, orange-reds, and brownish-oranges. In his *Women of Algiers,* of 1834, with its very deep emerald green offset by luminous white, almost gaudy gold and reds ranging from faint pinks to deep madder, his romantic palette is seen in all its splendor. The painting has delighted artists and colorists of the twentieth century for its subtle weaving of shapes and colors.

*Eug. Delacroix
1848*

EMERALD

ALGIERS GREEN

FEZ YELLOW

MARRAKECH RED

LIGHT BLUE

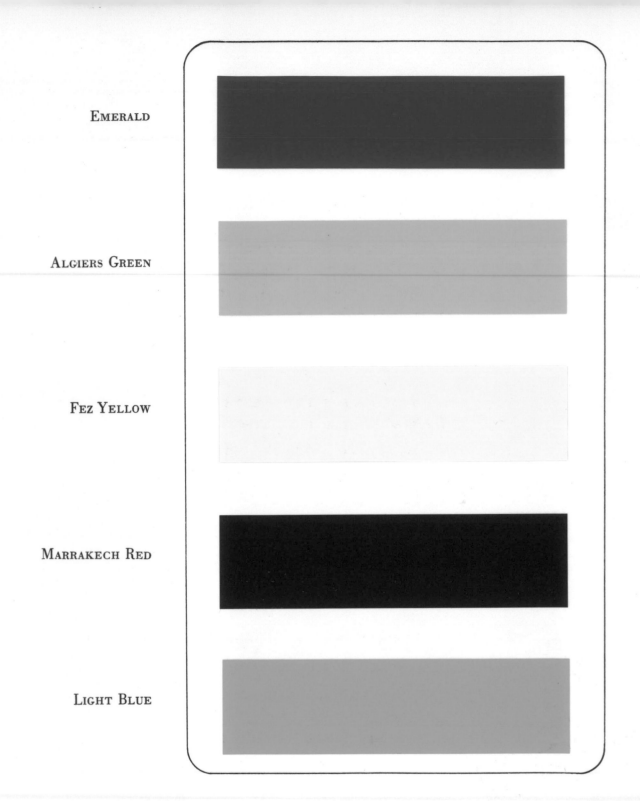

GAUGUIN'S PALETTE

"CLOISONNISM," which consists of surrounding areas of pure color with heavy, sinuous contours, is readily associated with its most famous originator and practitioner, Paul Gauguin. Like Van Gogh, Gauguin liberated color from its representational service. He sought "art as an abstraction" in a non-naturalistic style with an emphasis on bold, decorative outline and flat, bright colors.

Gauguin's palette is that of a decorative symbolist, who strove to render his feelings directly by the abstract equivalent on canvas of line, shade, and above all color. It is paradoxical proof of Gauguin's freely inventive color symbolism that his Brittany pictures are lighter in value than his South Seas canvases painted in the brilliance of the southern sun.

Tahiti, the island of Gauguin's refuge from civilization in the 1890's, provided the perfect setting for the maturation of his intense colors. In the brilliant sun of the South Seas, Gauguin's unique palette of non-primary hues — most notably pinks, mauves, oranges, and violets — reached full intensity. Unlike the Impressionists, Gauguin used mixed, rather than primary colors, and chose allied, rather than contrasting, color harmonies. In his use of inventive color juxtapositions, Gauguin anticipated the color cult of the Fauves and many twentieth-century color schemes.

PINK

ORANGE

MAUVE

VIOLET

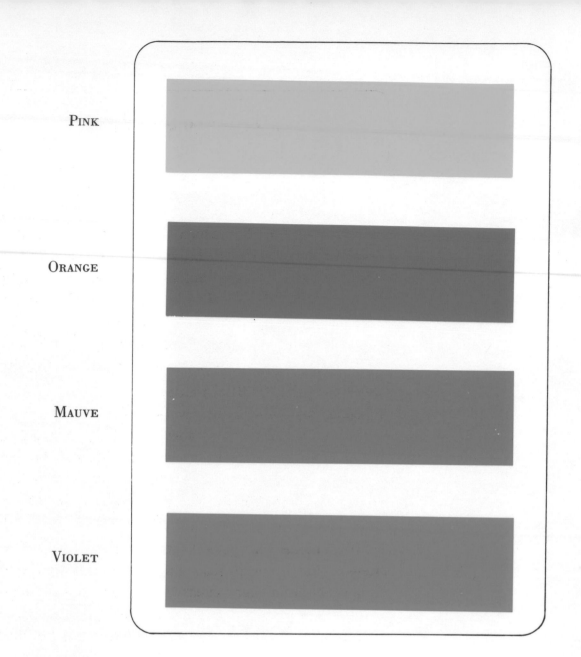

MONET'S PALETTE

CLAUDE Monet most completely epitomized the ideas and works that were to be grouped under the Impressionist banner in the 1870's. Above all, Monet attempted to capture on the painted canvas his impression of nature's colors in constantly changing light. Often, he was exasperated because he painted too slowly to achieve "instantaneity" of color, namely the "envelope" of colored light that momentarily unifies a scene.

Monet painted many famous series of subjects like the Rouen Cathedral as seen under different light effects. Changing canvases with the light, Monet followed the hours of the day from the early morning with the façade in misty shadow, to the afternoon when it is flooded with sunlight, and finally to the end of the day when the disappearing sunset weaves the weathered stonework into a strong fabric of burnt orange and blue.

Monet's palette, from which black and white were removed, consisted of the brightest, unmixed pigments of the solar spectrum: yellows, oranges, vermilions, lakes, reds, violets, blues, and intense greens such as Veronese and emerald. For intensity, Monet concentrated on the juxtaposition of complementaries. Hence, his passion for poppies and red parasols in green fields, or orange sunsets reflected in blue water.

Shadow Violet

Parasol Red

Cathedral Blue

Mediterranean

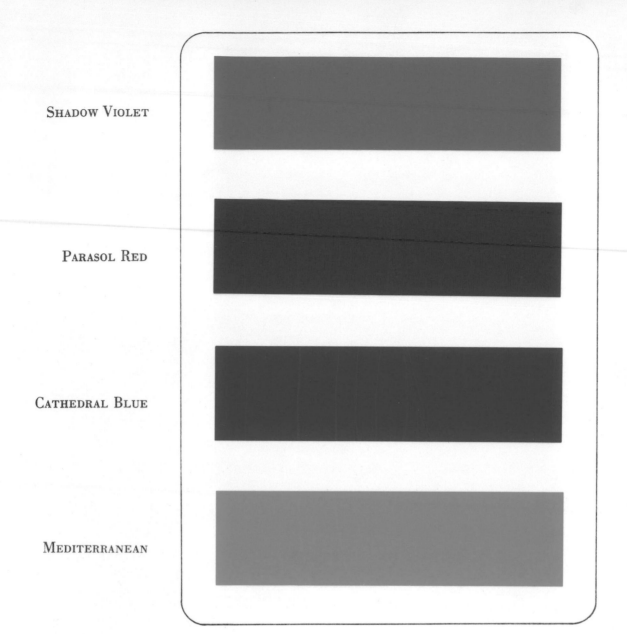

RENOIR COLORS & IMPRESSIONISM

I T IS difficult not to single out the two French painters Renoir and Monet as the men most responsible for the development of Impressionism.

Shortly after the Franco-Prussian War, the two men began to explore the limitless potentials in rendering atmospheric effects with small broken applications of pure color. They took a significant hint from the Gobelin Director Chevreul's treatise on color, particularly the formulation of simultaneous contrasts. M. Chevreul pointed out that every color tends to throw its complementary cast on the color next to it. By using this theory, the Impressionists revolutionized the rendering of light and air effects. What Chevreul pointed out was indeed a fact: green grass and yellow haystacks will cast violet shades; red will tend to give the impression of green or green-blue effects on objects near it, and so on. Values of black and white were no longer needed to render light and shade effects. All was magically transformed with color. All was possible with color.

Renoir, going beyond Impressionism towards his own personal vision, never lost his love for the luminous colors he used in his Impressionist period. The colors which we have designated as Renoir colors are typical of the sensuous charm of his palette.

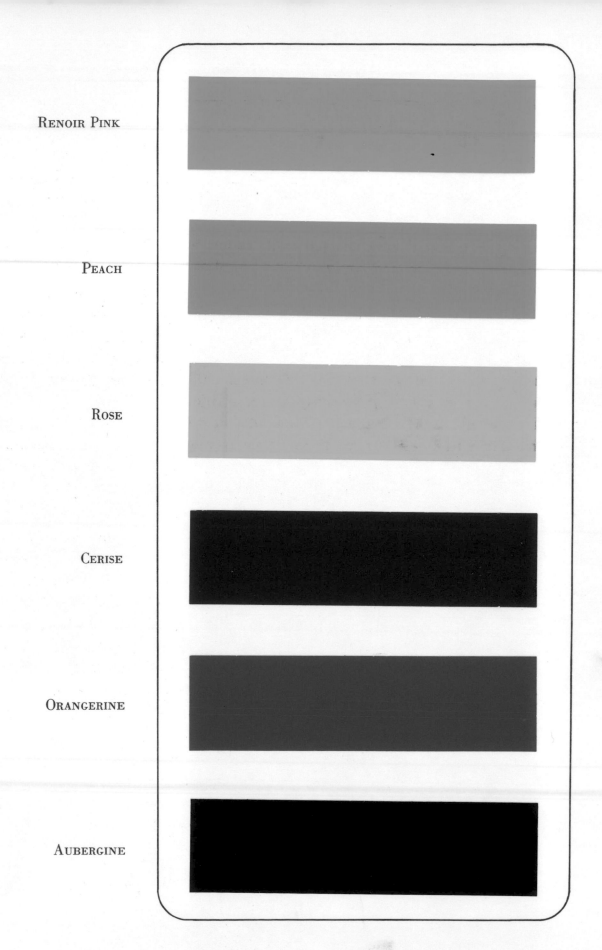

RENOIR PINK

PEACH

ROSE

CERISE

ORANGERINE

AUBERGINE

TIFFANY COLORS

AT THE turn of the twentieth century, there was a considerable revolution in the arts which came to be known as Art Nouveau. The style, characterized by an asymmetrically undulating line, has bequeathed to us a wealth of artifacts in the decorative arts. Entrancingly beautiful, the opalescent glass of Louis C. Tiffany is a superb record of the entirely different range of unconventional colors popular during the Art Nouveau period.

Setting out to be the first American industrial artist to fuse art and life and to produce "good art in our times" for everyone to enjoy, Tiffany established in 1893 the first of his own glass furnaces in Long Island. Tiffany's blown glass, known as "Favrile," shortly afterwards became world-famous.

Tiffany's revolutionary technique carefully controlled the way in which layers of colored glass were made to flow either transparently or opaquely over each other. In Tiffany's high-stemmed transparent pastel-colored glass and as well in his bowls of the deepest hues with layers of glass laid one on top of the other, the effect was almost mystical. The metallic irridescence of Tiffany glass reveals a preference for pearly and unconventional colors. Milky white, olive green, muted browns and yellows, orange-reds, pink, turquoise and various shades of violet are typical. Marbelized combinations of a myriad of these colors produced a rich, velvety effect while following Tiffany's precept of avoiding glaring contrasts of color.

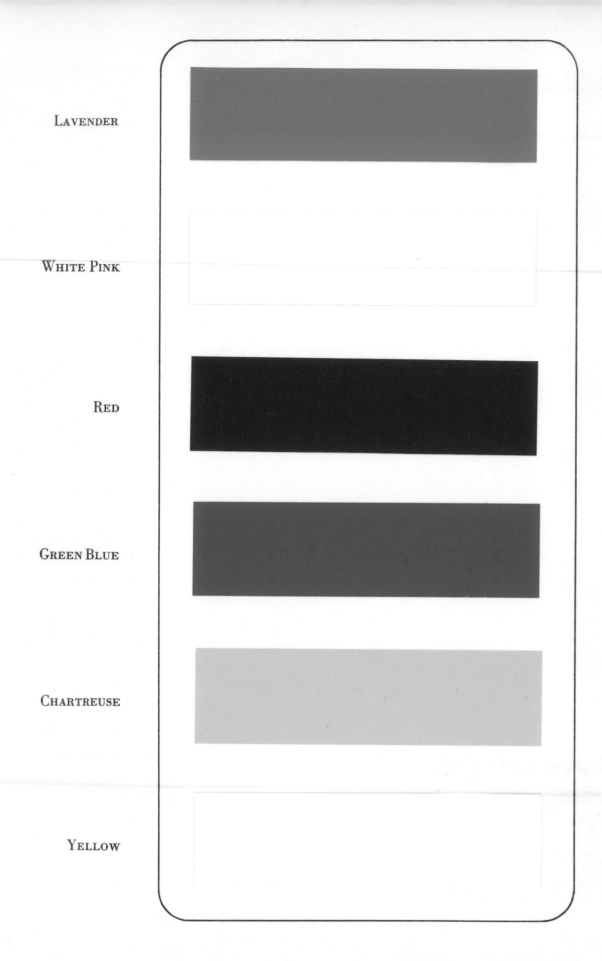

LAVENDER

WHITE PINK

RED

GREEN BLUE

CHARTREUSE

YELLOW

SEURAT'S POINTILLIST PALETTE

The pointillist painter George Seurat (1859–1891) developed a theory of painting based on the use of pure color, which was far more self-conscious and more scientific than that of the Impressionists. Seurat's pointillism—juxtaposed minute dots of pure color—rendered objects and space by systematically using recently discovered principles of optics. The pointillist method was largely based on two laws of color optics formulated by Michel-Eugène Chevreul, a chemist and physicist who became Director of Dyeing at the Manufacture de Gobelins in 1824. Chevreul had correctly pointed out in his Law of Simultaneous Contrasts that a mutual enhancement of color intensity will result from a juxtaposition of complementaries. Red does become more intensely red, for instance, green more fiercely green, when these two are contiguous. In his Law of Successive Contrasts, Chevreul pointed out the optical sensation of a complementary halo that gradually appears to surround an intense hue. This complementary glow is superimposed on surrounding, weaker colors. For example, gray becomes greenish when juxtaposed to red, and reddish in close relation to green.

In his painting in the 1880s, Seurat achieved optical tone effects based on these laws. His analysis of the color of an object took into account several factors: the color of the object in white light (its local color); the color of light falling on it (a warm yellow if the object were in sunlight); the color reflected onto the object by other objects; and the color induced by contrast with neighboring hues. Seurat's work, which is most often noted for its frozen, friezelike atmospheric qualities, in large part achieves its powerful effects through color conceived not in terms of pigment but in terms of the optical mixtures of light.

For the designer, and particularly for the textile designer, the pointillist palette of optical mixtures offers endless possibilities.

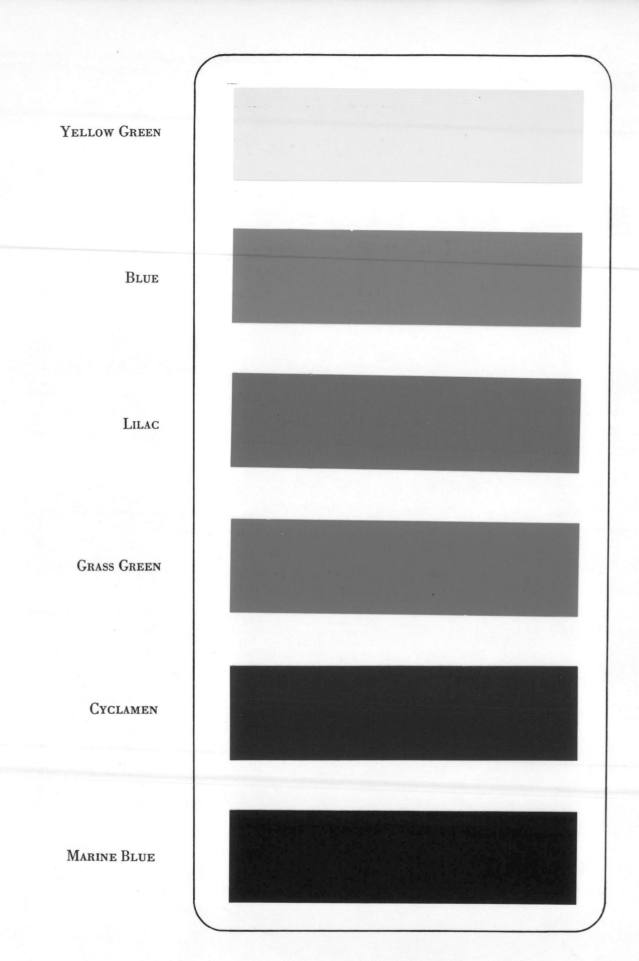

YELLOW GREEN

BLUE

LILAC

GRASS GREEN

CYCLAMEN

MARINE BLUE

WILLIAM MORRIS'S NATURE COLORS

William Morris (1834–1896), English poet, artist, and socialist, was above all a master at enriching a surface with meandering patterns of florals and neogothic clusters of woodland colors. A maker of furniture, stained glass, books, wallpapers, printed and woven textiles, Morris was the exemplar of the craftsman-artist, who combined designing with the successful running of a factory from 1861 until his death in 1896. As the leader of the British Arts and Crafts Movement, Morris tried to see that well-designed goods of every kind were available to all levels of society.

Morris was a firm advocate of natural dyes in an era that had just discovered synthetic ones. In his essay "Of Dyeing as an Art," which appeared in the catalog of the Arts and Crafts Exhibition Society of 1889, he wrote that with the discovery of aniline dyes (1856) there had come about "an absolute divorce between the *commercial process* and the *art* of dyeing so that any one wanting to produce dyed textiles of any artistic quality in them must entirely forego the modern and commercial methods in favor of those which are as old as Pliny, who speaks of them as being old in his time."

We know that Morris did many experiments according to the methods of the ancients. He experimented with the four basic colors—blue, red, yellow, and brown—needed for dyeing. From Greece, he obtained *kermes*, a red dye made from the bodies of insects. This yielded a particularly fine shade of red. He boiled poplar and osier twigs, which gave, in his words, "a good strong yellow." Brown he got from the roots of the walnut tree, blue from indigo.

Morris's first wallpapers, "The Daisy," "The Trellis," and "The Fruit," date from 1864. They heralded over seventy patterns for wallpapers, chintzes, and woven cloths made in the following thirty years. During this time, the name Morris, and particularly Morris chintzes, became household words of prestige among the middle classes in both England and the United States. The colors for the Morris palette—all strong forest hues—are chosen from these last thirty years. The warm appeal of this woodland color cluster explains in part why Morris's chintzes and wallpapers were so popular.

INDIGO

PALE ORANGE

GREEN GRAY

DEEP GREEN

BROWNED ORANGE

GARNET RED

M ATISSE is known as the greatest colorist even in a period (1890-1914) which produced immense creative and technical color achievements. To an intense emotional feeling for color, he brought a disciplined intellect. To the life of the spirit, he brought the leaven of the mind. The spell-like enchantment of his work was not confined to the work alone. His colors have the astounding gift of evoking a genuine experience in the spectator.

In a way, it is presumptuous to indicate a "Matisse" palette. He used all the pure and happy primary colors in such a way that they become enchanting and joyful expressions of a great man's inner life. Even pure black becomes a lively, expressive color in his hands. We have selected five primary colors in the hue and value that Matisse chose.

Nude Figure Blue

Joy Orange

Paper Pink

Cut-out Magenta

Collage Green

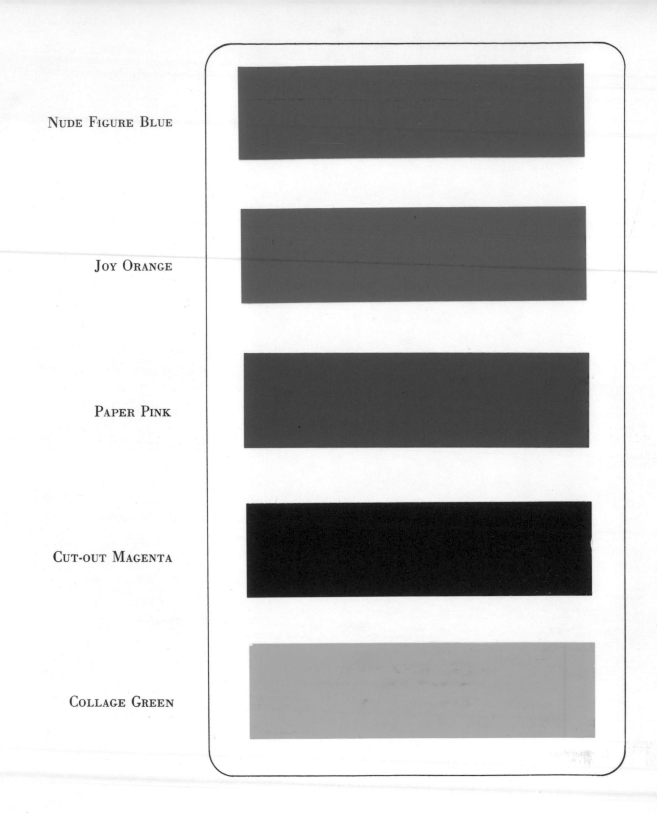

PAUL POIRET'S
HAUTE COUTURE COLORS

Paul Poiret (1880–1944), the leading French couturier who epitomized the lavish chic of pre–World War I Paris, did much to bring an end to corseted fashions and to washed-out blues, suppressed pinks, morbid mauves, and funereal blacks of the late nineteenth century. Poiret, who advocated colors that would be "like a blow in the face," used brilliant reds (often in combination with purples), gold, emerald and lime greens, and deep blues in supple, soft fabrics like charmeuse, georgette, and chiffon. In his heyday, from 1903 to 1914, Poiret's colorful outfits did much to assure that haute couture, established at the Exposition Universelle of 1900, would choose from a wide and vivid range of colors.

Exotic and *artistic*, the two adjectives most frequently applied to Poiret's work, suggest two important influences on his work. One strong influence was the orientalism found in Persian colorings and shapes. Poiret's famous belted, knee-length "minaret" tunic with wired flaring edges over a slim silhouette, his harem or trouser skirts, and his use of embroideries all stem from his love of Persian miniatures. An equally important influence on Poiret was the Diaghilev Ballet, the sensation of Paris in 1909. The sets of Leon Bakst brought a burst of orientalism and color the likes of which Paris had not seen before.

The colors chosen to represent Poiret's lavish design ensembles are all strong, "solid" (as Poiret himself called the hues he chose) tones: cerise, purple, turban gold, emerald green, Prussian blue, browned orange, and lime green.

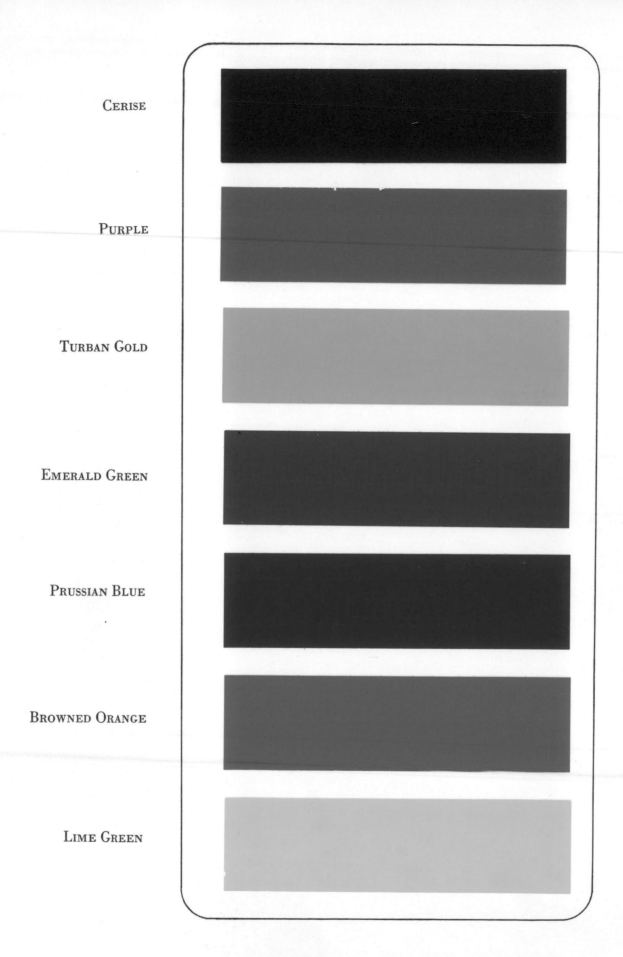

CERISE

PURPLE

TURBAN GOLD

EMERALD GREEN

PRUSSIAN BLUE

BROWNED ORANGE

LIME GREEN

ART DECO COLORS

THE STYLE now popularly known as Art Deco was first presented to the world at the great Paris exhibition of 1925 — L'Exposition Internationales des Arts Décoratifs et Industriels Modernes. Hard, rectilinear, precisely defined geometric shapes typified this new style that was to dominate European and American design of the late 1920's and 1930's.

Art Deco derived its palette directly from the art sources which originally influenced its formation. Ancient Egyptian art, the art of the American Indians, Cubism, Bauhaus design, and the Russian ballet all contributed to an Art Deco palette. Ancient Egypt's influence can be seen in the extensive use of ocher and gold. This can still be observed in our fast-disappearing Egyptian cinema palaces as well as in the zigzag motif which has been revived in graphic arts today. From the American Indians came such desert sun colors of the Art Deco style as the coral red of coral beads. Also Indian inspired are the off-white of undyed wool and Aztec jade green. From Cubism and Bauhaus design came a distinct preference for a very limited and basically monotone palette, for rarely does an Art Deco design use more than one vivid color at a time. From the riot of strong Russian ballet costume colors, the practitioners of the Art Deco style adopted but one hue — orange — and used it to the hilt.

Basically, the Art Deco palette is a restrained one of soft, almost non-descript colors like smoky white, chrome, gold, pale yellow. In this palette that leaves more room for refinement of form than chromatic play are two vivid, almost lurid colors, Art Deco Orange and Aztec Jade Green.

ORANGE

JADE GREEN

CORAL RED

SMOKY WHITE

YELLOW

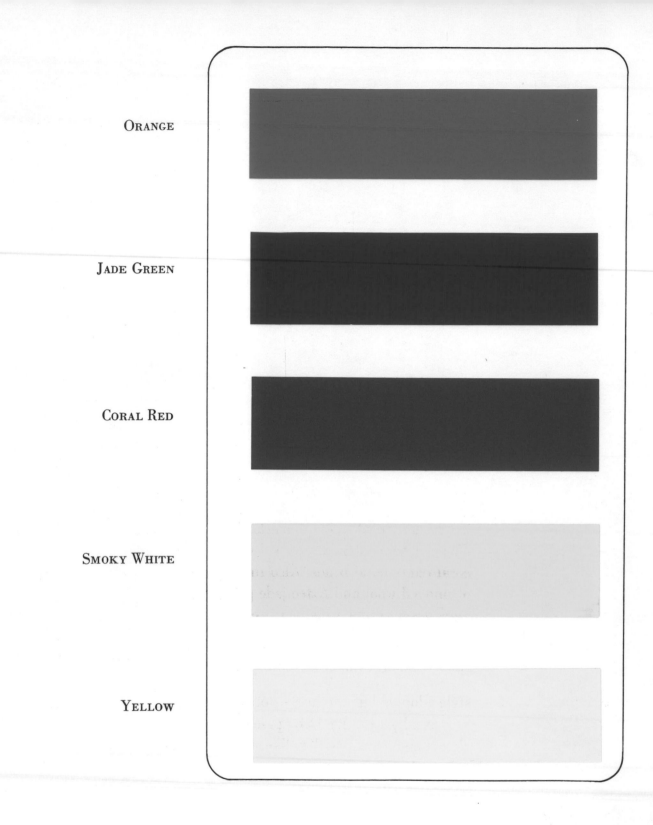

BONNARD'S LITHOGRAPH COLORS

When the great exposition of Japanese prints opened in 1890 at the Beaux Arts in Paris, it had an electrifying influence on Pierre Bonnard and his friend Edouard Vuillard. Then in their early twenties, the two painters responded immediately to the new world of Kakemonos and flat colors. In the period after his discovery of Hokusai, Utamaro, and other Japanese print makers, Bonnard, working quietly and modestly, created a large number of lithographs for posters, magazines, music albums, and for books. His notorious poster "France Champagne," one of his first lithographs, appeared on the walls of Paris, bringing a much impressed Toulouse-Lautrec to call on Bonnard. The medium had a peculiar fascination for him, and its disciplines and special demands were met by the artist. Each of his lithographs bears the imprint of the master—direct, simple, fresh—as if made in the moment. Often working with as few as two or three colors, Bonnard soon evolved an essentially personal palette. He frequently used the device of accenting a large, pale surface with a strong dark note—for example, reddish black printed on an ivory ground. He also used two pale off-monochromatic shades which interact with each other. The colors which appeared most frequently in his prints were *reddish black, bottle green, sulfur green, orange beige, rose beige, pink ochre,* and *ivory.*

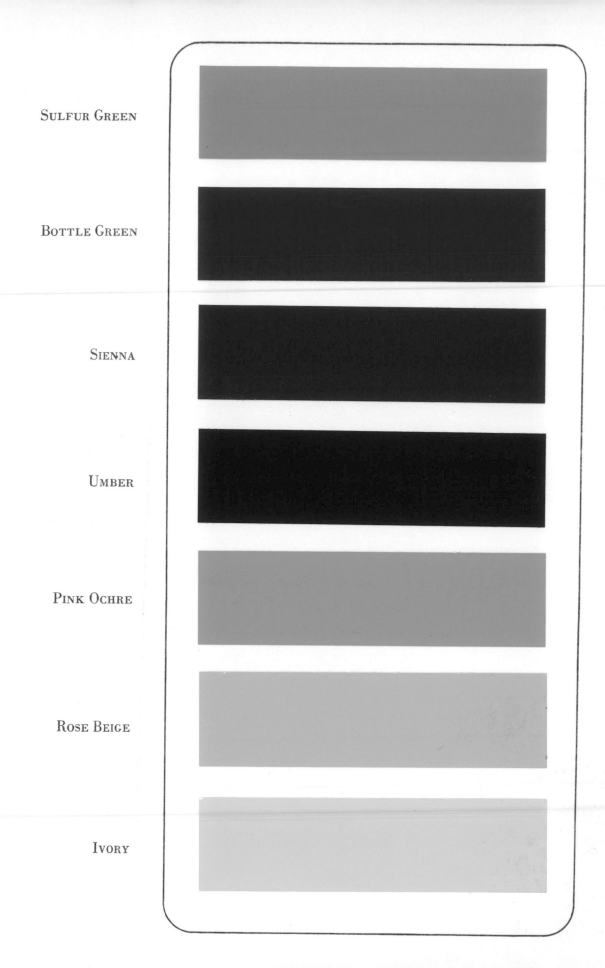

SULFUR GREEN

BOTTLE GREEN

SIENNA

UMBER

PINK OCHRE

ROSE BEIGE

IVORY

BRAQUE'S PALETTE

TO GEORGES BRAQUE, undoubtedly the greatest twentieth-century still-life painter, belongs a grave dusk-like palette of black, browns, grayed pinks and blues, and opaque greens. Braque was more concerned with space than color. "All my life my great concern has been to paint space," he once declared. It was while exploring Cubist space — a space determined not by conventional perspective by seeing objects from many vantage points — that Braque evolved his gentle palette of soft, velvet grayed contrasts. In a sense, Braque's *grisaille* palette of the softest variations of buffs, grays, browns, pinks, greens, and blues was evolved precisely because vivid colors would have interfered with the cubist's concern with space.

Braque, along with Picasso, was the prime generator of the Cubist Movement. By 1911 the fragmented, volumetric, compact style of Analytical Cubism was formed. But a year or two later the synthetic phase of cubism came into being. In Synthetic Cubism planes are larger and simpler and aligned more directly with the picture frame. The subjects one invariably finds in Braque's works are musical instruments and scores, furniture, bottles, and other everyday objects of the typical French bourgeois interior. The palette represents one of an unruffled harmony of wonderful browns — the cubist *café au lait* (brownish orange) khaki, walnut, and deep chocolate—grayed blues and pinks, and opaque greens. Black ("Black is a very rich color," Braque once said) plays a key role both in outlining and in large areas.

Chosen to represent Braque palette are three shades of brown — the cubist *café au lait,* a sandalwood, and a deep chocolate —a cream buff, a grayed pink, and a grayed Cezannesque green.

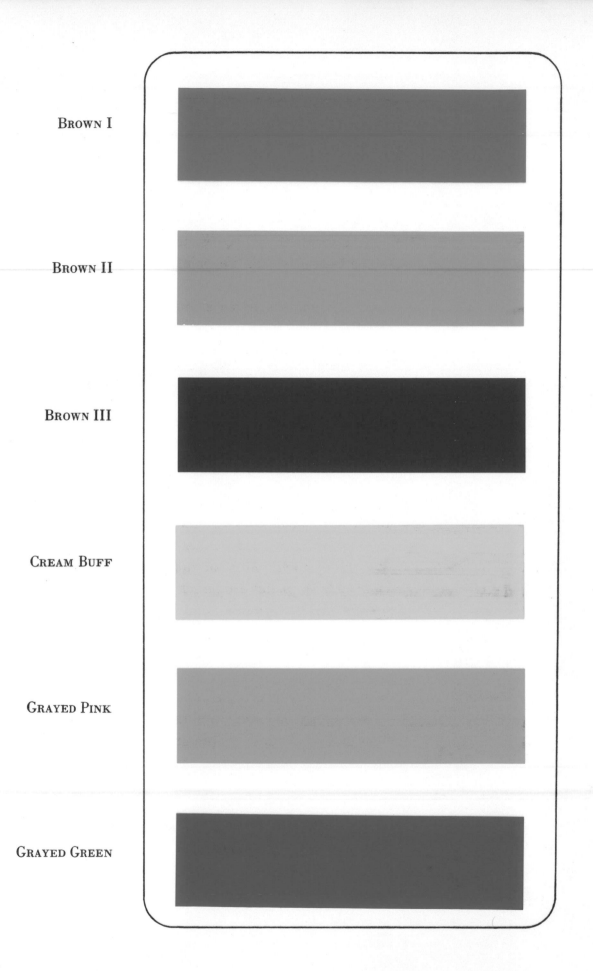

BROWN I

BROWN II

BROWN III

CREAM BUFF

GRAYED PINK

GRAYED GREEN

ALBERS'S COLORS

Josef Albers played a large part in twentieth-century color history. In his varied roles of experimental teacher, theoretician, and perceptual painter he focused on the relativity, the instability, and the wealth of ambiguity and emotive content of color relationships that make up the complexities of human visual experience.

From 1923 to 1933, Albers pioneered what was to become the famous experimental "foundations" course at the Bauhaus.

In 1949, Albers began a profound investigation of color form that he entitled "Homage to the Square."

In "Homage to the Square," Albers established compositions of three or four squares. Each of the squares nests in another and each is composed of just one unmixed color evenly applied with a palette knife. The series is really an "homage" to color because it demonstrates how color can undergo change because of its environment. Moreover, in "Homage to the Square," Albers shows how color in the form of the square acts as a means of plastic organization: squares move back and forth, in and out, up and down, enlarge and diminish, all because of color effects.

Theoretical implications of Albers's visual researches are set forth in his monumental text *Interaction of Colors* (1963). There is one distinctive difference between this book and all others on the science of colors: it contains more psychology of color, more visual training than abstract theory. In the introduction, Albers explains his essentially experimental way of studying and teaching color:

> In visual perception a color is almost never seen as it really is—as it physically is. This fact makes color the most relative medium in art. In order to use color effectively, it is necessary to recognize that color deceives continually.

Albers's perceptual painting and his research for *Interaction of Colors* make use of many principles of Gestalt psychology. The most important of these is the overwhelming influence of context upon perception. Albers's visual researches demonstrate how a limited number of colors change and become modified by their environment and can thus achieve an astounding number of effects.

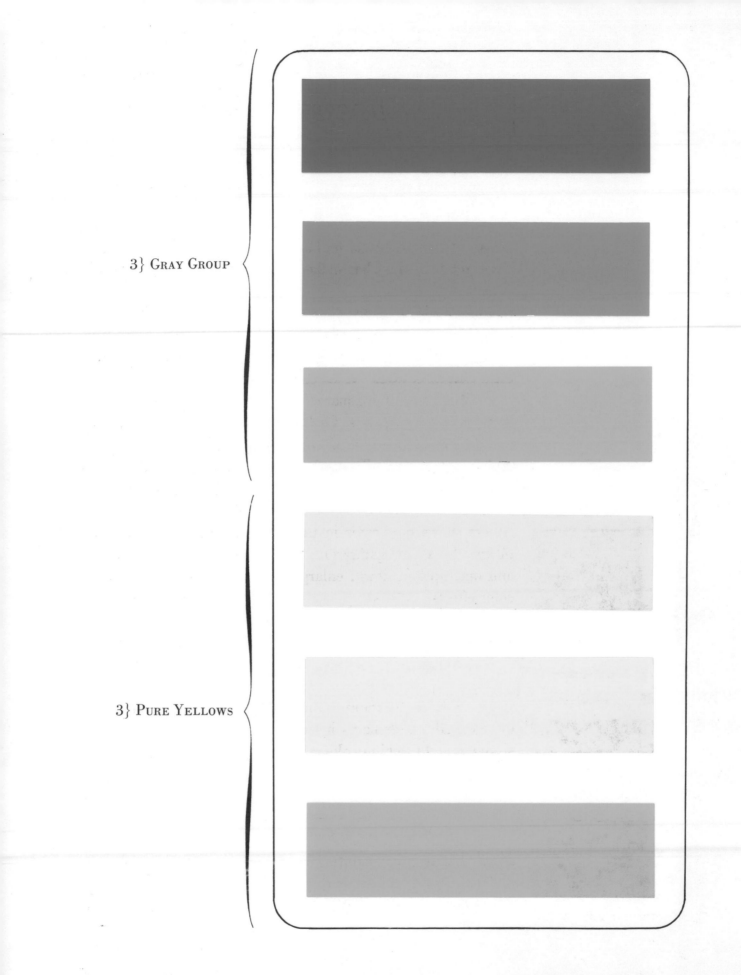

3} Gray Group

3} Pure Yellows

POP ART COLORS

I N THE early 1960's Pop Art first mesmerized and then outraged the American public by its glorification of the commonplace. Reacting against the highly personal art of abstract expressionism, Pop artists offered a super-realistic art which in both subject and style was highly depersonalized. Mass-produced images, and objects from repeated faces of a photographed Marilyn Monroe to Campbell soup cans, were shown in the slick, visual vocabularly of America's commercial culture.

Fittingly enough, the Pop artists chose the standardized, harsh look of the raw primaries of printer's red, yellow and blue or the colors from commercial products themselves. Imitating the crassest of commercial illustration, Roy Lichtenstein, the Pop artist of comic strip fame, enlarged Ben-Day dots in raw primaries. James Rosenquist, infatuated with Franco-American spaghetti or a magazine photograph of a Florida orange, used the most bilious of commercial hues. Claes Oldenburg's sculpture of gigantic kitchen appliances in vinyl celebrated the slick, wet colors of the plastic age. And Andy Warhol, the daddy of Pop, mimicked the hygienic, impersonal colors of commercial art in his famous silk-screened Brillo boxes.

The Pop Art palette is composed of colors of two orders. There is the group of raw primaries seen in Warhol's Brillo boxes and many of Lichtenstein's comic scripts. Secondly, there are the colors of a plastic and chrome-dominated society. Our palette shows four of the second variety of colors: a car bumper chrome, a turquoise plastic dish color, an abrasive pumpkin yellow, and a baby pink flesh tone.

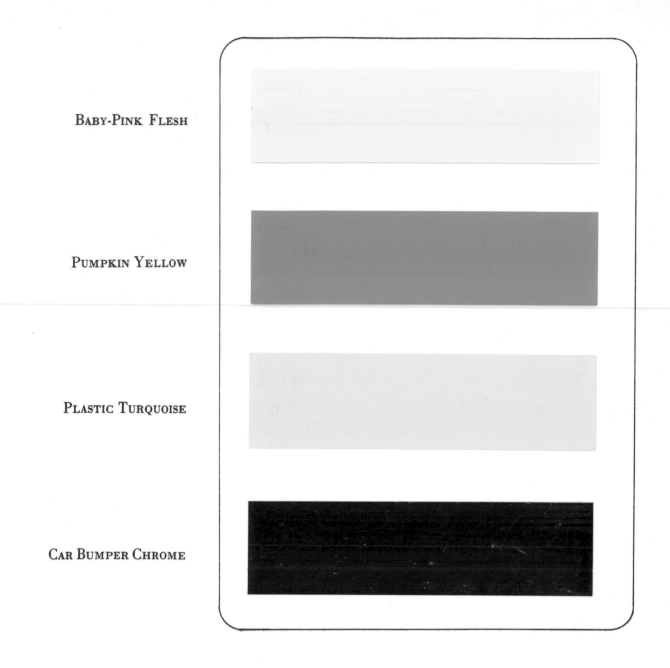

BABY-PINK FLESH

PUMPKIN YELLOW

PLASTIC TURQUOISE

CAR BUMPER CHROME

Sheila Hicks, a contemporary American artist, is the leader in innovating tapestry and textile art. Her role is similar to that of Marcel Duchamp within her field in that she has presented unprecedented works using fiber and textile.

Her experiments during the last twenty years have gone beyond the boundaries previously established and have opened new frontiers of research.

Having studied color with Josef Albers, the influence of his teaching has made a great impact on her utilizing color in a fresh and unexpected way. One color palette often employed is that of very subtle, close harmonies, often nearly monochromatic, as seen in the Ford Foundation building, New York (honey-colored Lyons silk), or on all of the Air France Boeing 747 lounges (natural Chinese raw silk).

Her color palette derives in part from her travel throughout the world and notably from her experience in textile workshops in Mexico, Morocco, and India. The colors selected show a range of earth tones from natural to a rusty terra cotta, in combination with "hot" colors—two Mexican pinks and an orange from Bangalore.

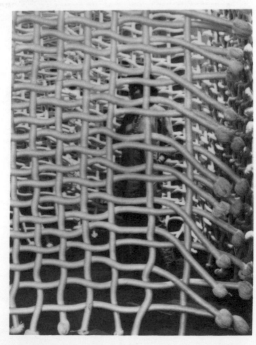

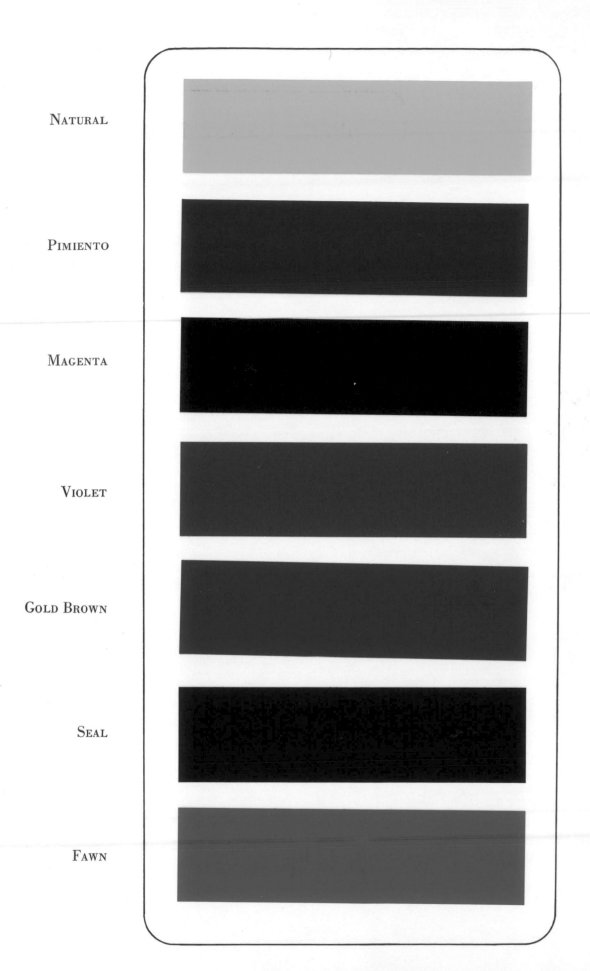

NATURAL

PIMIENTO

MAGENTA

VIOLET

GOLD BROWN

SEAL

FAWN

as concept, as data, as interface, as digital-organic growth, as mutation or insertion. Furnish illustrates a Babel of form that is breathtaking in its diversity from flatpack baroque or postmodern porcelain to strange neo-organic chimeras. Hybridisation and appropriation are key themes – opening up all the borders means abandoning rules of aesthetics and genre distinctions. Mixing hi-tech with retro elements, building in historical narrative or bootlegging the designs of others are all permissible. Only the laws of physics still apply: If you want to make a chair then it has to be structurally sound or you won't be able to sit on it and it can't therefore be a chair (unless of course it is a concept masquerading as a chair).

Furnish also explores the new hybrid nature of occupied spaces. Our homes, we are told, are supposed to be turning into high-tech ambient interfaces filled with sensors, touch screens and smart materials. But instead of looking like the now hackneyed futuristic predictions based on Stanley Kubrick's or Gene Roddenberry's visions, we seem to be busy morphing them into customised playgrounds full of fantasy furniture, pimped heirlooms and surround sound; a whole panoply of styles and technologies is turning 'our house' into a 'funhouse'. More and more public and commercial spaces too are being devoted to playfully interactive or fully fledged fantasy environments: designers are now expected to deliver more to lounge areas, clubs, and trade fairs than a few chairs, screens and decorative elements. It could be argued that developments in lavishly detailed and highly realistic special effects in the film media have raised the bar considerably when it comes to consumer expectations. Why limit our future environments to "2001" and "Star Trek" when we have a whole wealth of digitally enhanced visual imagery to draw upon?

Beyond film, the digital revolution in general has a lot to do with a growing interest in the sensuality of objects, materials and in plain old 3-D space. Now we have got used to incredibly fast and easy access to a sophisticated breadth of dynamic visual effects on our computers as well as the big screen, creatives are taking theoretical and stylistic lessons learned in 2-D and applying them back in the real world where more of our senses can be satisfied by the experience in 3-D.

Another key contemporary theme is individuality: Manufacturers are starting to realise that individual attention amidst all that mass production is a seductive selling tool and designers too seem to yearn for a sense of individuality by disengaging from the industrial ethic. Ironically, or perhaps interestingly, some of the very tools that facilitate this new individuality are being provided by technological advances in industry itself. Rapid Prototyping, for example, is an industrial process that lends itself immediately to limited editions, customisation and one-offs. Here the design itself is a piece of computer data. Adapting the design before each product is made is a relatively simple exercise. Thus this new manufacturing technique – although in its infancy and still quite expensive – has the potential to facilitate both customised individual pieces and perfect replicas on a large scale. In addition, it allows for local production and a concurrent reduction in transport costs: Send the product file to a rapid processing production plant anywhere in the world and you have local manufacture.

Individuality and singularity implies rarity, which in turn breeds desire. Ours is a powerfully visual culture where we fetishise fashion, beauty and even furniture. The collectability of contemporary design objects has increased dramatically over the past decade. It is not just rare Eames chairs that are reaching astronomical sums at auction or occupying expensive gallery square footage, but a new breed of limited edition, high finish design pieces as well. Top 'name' designers are often producing commercial work for manufacturers and limited editions for their galleries in parallel, feeding both the collector and consumer market alike. Yes, this is an elite market buoyed by mediaphilic imagery and hype, but it does raise interesting questions as to the nature of the relationship between a certain kind of design and fine art.

Certainly, and thanks in no small part to the influence of the Dutch design company Droog founded in 1993, there are areas of design which seem to be functioning more and more at an 'art' level. Pieces are being created which address issues, explore concepts and express thoughts that seem to have very little to do with commercial or utilitarian application. This critical and questioning aspect of what has come to be called 'conceptual design' is appropriated from what is traditionally an artistic approach. It often provides welcome pauses and punctuations within the flood of creation for visual consumption – even if the results risk ending up as relatively banal one-liners.

Finally, Furnish is about trying to capture a certain Zeitgeist and by no means intended to be a definitive analysis. In talking about recent history, it is unavoidable that certain protagonists have been omitted who may later transpire to have played decisive roles, and for others that were included to turn out to be only momentary (albeit very bright) blips on the radar. Little distinction has been made between disciplines as well. It may seem irreverent to some to juxtapose fine art installations, for example, with trade fair stands and rough prototypes, but that seems to go with the territory of the blurred boundaries we are experiencing. Likewise, there are relevant issues such as sustainability and mobility that remain barely addressed here due to reasons of space. Nevertheless, the wealth of ideas and breadth of scope represented by all the artists, designers and architects featured in Furnish will hopefully provide much food for thought, discussion and inspiration until the next volume. Enjoy.

Peter Andersson
Tilt
chair for disobedient behaviour
Client: NC Möbler AB

4

FURNISH

Furniture and Interior Design for the 21st Century

Die Gestalten Verlag

"Don't we want irony?
A sense of humour and the wisdom that nothing lasts forever?"

Gaetano Pesce

We have entered an age where the boundaries between creative disciplines have become noticeably porous and where new technologies, materials and processes alter our environments with greater frequency than ever before. The rules that govern how we furnish our living spaces are in the process of being rewritten – at least for those living within the technological development bubble. Furnish seeks to document new work from pioneering designers, artists and architects exploring new domestic territories. This work moves beyond the pre-kindergarten aesthetic of 'blobjects' or the stripped down worthiness of 'new functionalism' of the nineties and signals a more developed sense of playfulness and irreverent thrift, as well as the beginnings of a new vocabulary of form.

Design has become a catch-all term that can no longer be pigeonholed into discrete disciplines. In fact, all the creative fields are in sore need of a new vocabulary to match the vagaries of its protagonists. It is not unusual, for example, to find architects engineering tables, artists designing tree houses, graphic designers tuning sofas and jaded industrial designers developing conceptual products that have nothing to do with practical function.

A discipline tends to be limited by its tools, but when we have access to affordable tools whose application capacity extends way beyond their original mandate, it is only natural to want to experiment. As computer sophistication and new technologies become increasing accessible to the individual, our capability to cross genres is dramatically expanding. Both consumers and designers are not just creating, editing and manipulating their own films, animations, websites and music, for example, but designing their own interiors, furniture, structures and objects as well with the aid of these technologies and the software that governs them. Far from making designers, artists or craftspeople redundant, this phenomenon seems only to be tending towards a further redundancy of categories and borders between disciplines. More of us are being more creative, and more creatives are broadening their fields of activity. Interestingly, the role of the skilled professional is not being eroded as a result, but their capacity for collaboration beyond the confines of their respective disciplines, should they choose to do so, has taken a quantum leap.

It is not just individuals who are discovering new opportunities beyond their conventional labels, object categories too are beginning to look increasingly wobbly: In this book alone, we find furniture as landscape; furniture

Peter Andersson
Rialto 437 Chair
Client: NC Möbler AB

Tilt
chair for disobedient behaviour
Client: NC Möbler AB

Peter Andersson
Solidarity Chair
prototype

Cédric Ragot Studio
'Compose It' Vase + 'La Chose' Stool +
'Cute Cut' Low Table Set
Client: Obvious + Obvious + Roche&Bobois

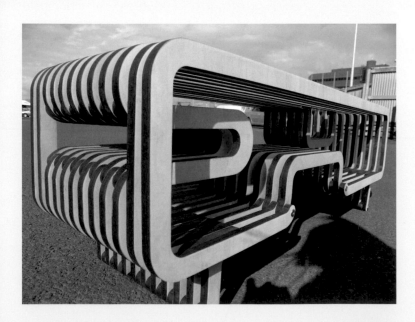

Studio Bility
Guðrún Lilja Gunnlaugsdóttir
<u>One Sheet</u>
light structured furniture laser-cut from one
sheet of plywood

Studio Bility
Guðrún Lilja Gunnlaugsdóttir
<u>Inner Beauty</u>
laser-cut plywood randomly put together so
the patterns within vary whilst the surface
stays the same

Studio Bility
Guðrún Lilja Gunnlaugsdóttir
<u>Inner Beauty</u>
laser-cut plywood randomly put together so
the patterns within vary whilst the surface
stays the same

12

Studio Bility
Guðrún Lilja Gunnlaugsdóttir
Flower Chair

Rocking Beauty
water jet-cut aluminium, plywood and macrolon
randomly assembled to create a barcode
pattern outside and a "mysterious garden" on
the inside

13

Alfredo Häberli
Empire
"A vertical sculpture full of books"
Client: Quodes, Netherlands

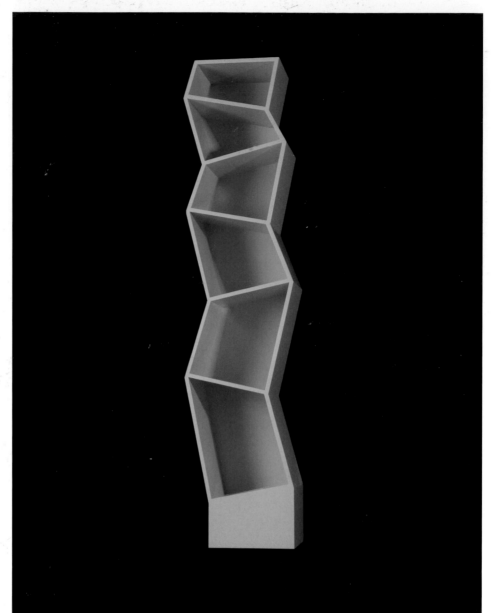

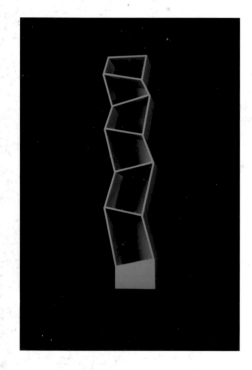

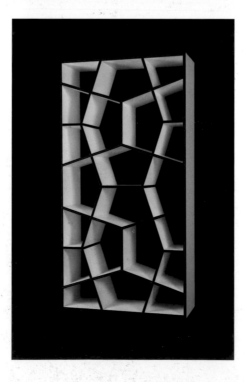

Alfredo Häberli
Empire
"A vertical sculpture full of books"

–left and opposite–
Pattern
modular, non-horizontal shelf unit based on
an irregular pentagonal repeat pattern
Client: Quodes, Netherlands

14

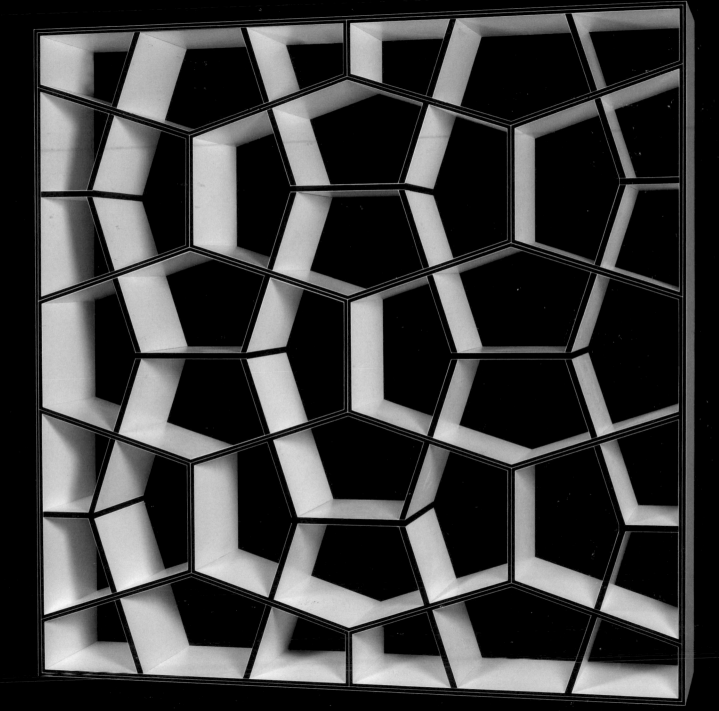

Studio Job
Job Smeets + Nynke Tynagel
The Perished Collection

"We inhabit the space between art and design, function and sculpture – the area where one thing floats into another."

Furniture ensemble exhibited in the Greenwich Village Design Art Gallery, London. Pieces are made from hardened tropical woods decorated with inlays depicting animal skeletons. It recalls Art Deco as well as Flemish art and is proposed as a precious collector's set. The inlays were cut using high-tech lasers and assembled by expert craftsmen. "We want to create a collection that is exclusive for the quality of the materials and techniques; haute couture products that will last at least a hundred years," say Studio Job.

Jaime Hayon
Mon Cirque Colection

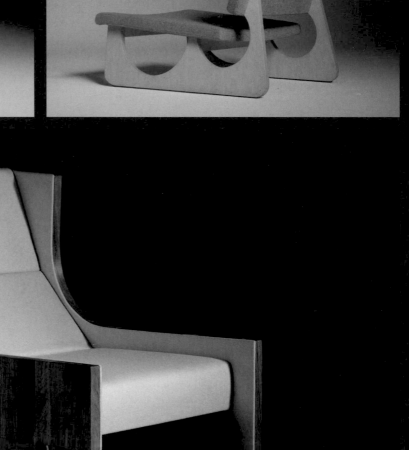

Autoban
Seyhan Özdemir + Sefer Çaglar

Autoban
Seyhan Özdemir + Sefer Çaglar
One-Armed Chair

e27
Iim Brauns, Hendrik Gackstatter + Fax Quintus
<u>Re-Move</u>
tuned Arne Jacobsen 3107 chair

–opposite–

Big-game
<u>L'Être Objet</u>
"Crossover between packaging and furniture
that can be interpreted both as a chair or as
a packaging for people."

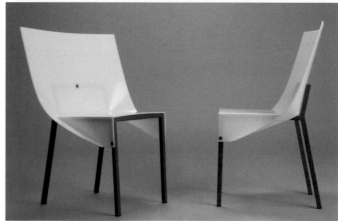

El Ultimo Grito
Roberto Feo + Rosario Furtado
<u>Miss Ramirez</u>
cork + latex chair limited edition
<u>'Marilyn, I can see your knickers' Chair</u>
initial prototype

Stefan Diez Industrial Design
Stefan Diez + Christophe de la Fontaine
Bent Stool + Lowseat
Client: Moroso

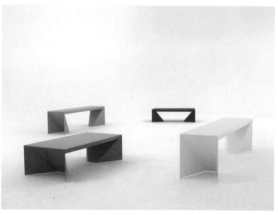

demacкerdesign
Matthias Demacker
Origami.Series
aluminium
Client: Van Esch

24

Form Us with Love
Origami Chair
lacquered birch plywood

Assa Ashuach
501 Chair GRP
limited edition of 50

Dejan Spasic
Wave Bench

Dejan Spasic
<u>Summer Chair</u>, <u>Spring Chairs</u>
<u>Wood Chair</u>, <u>Winter Chair</u>

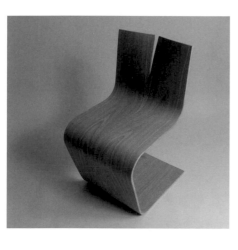

Duncan Bull
Felt It Too Armchair
prototype

28

Gitta Gschwendtner
<u>Up the Wall Lamp</u>
Client: Innermost
<u>Hugging Lamp</u>

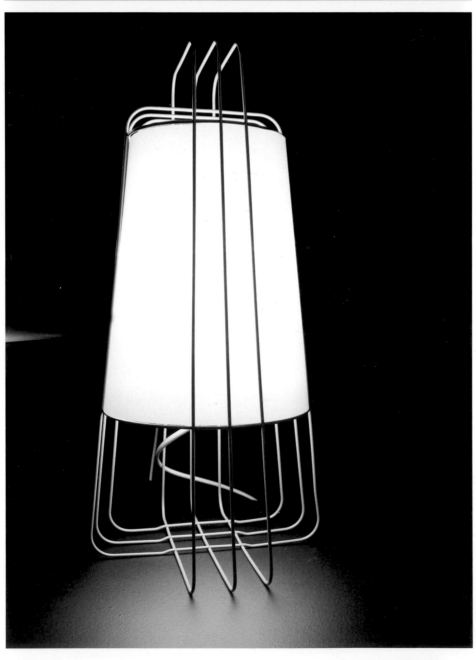

Big-game
<u>Moose</u>
wall-mounted plywood trophy made at Ecal
Client: Vlaemsch

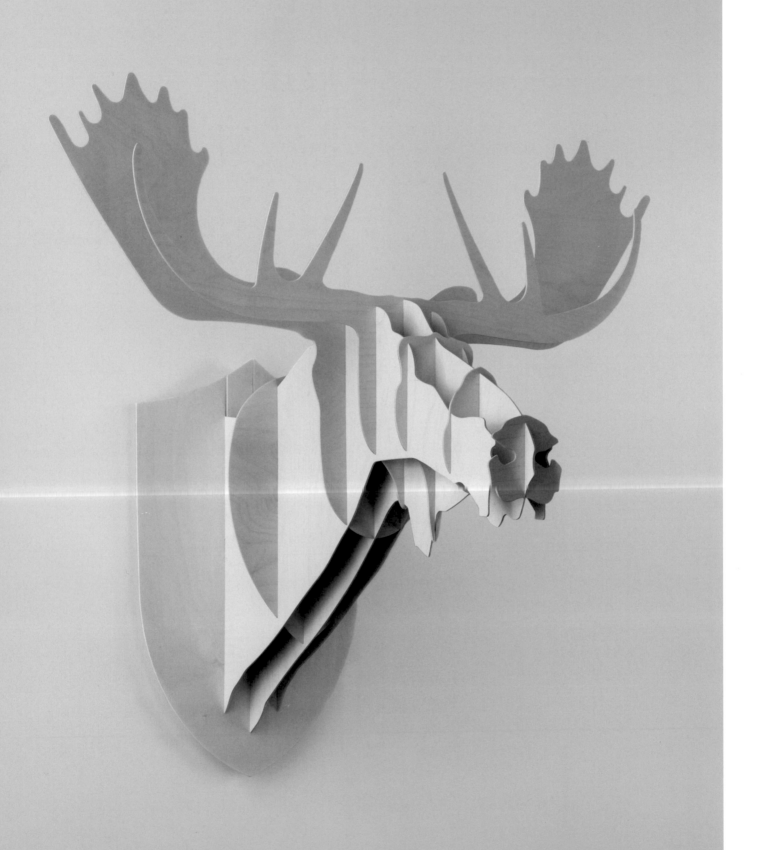

Big-game
<u>Pack Sweet Pack</u>
collection based on domestic and industrial
packaging

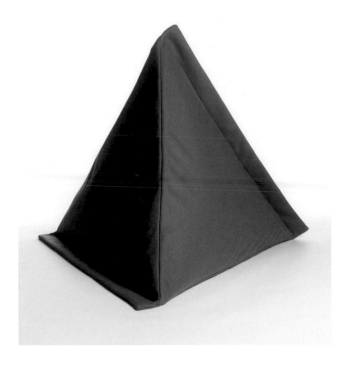

<u>Tetra</u>
seat inspired by the shape of industrial food
33   packaging

Big-game

[1] Styrene
expanded polystyrene lamp

[2] Site Lamp
"The lamp for building sites is a work of
genius: a simple halogen spotlight is fastened
to a bent steel tube that serves as a handle.
Big-game's version of it is made of stain-
less or gold-plated steel and is covered
by a fabric lampshade, which gives it a
domestic appearance. The formal references
of bourgeois furniture meet the temporary
beauty of the world of a building site."
Client: Mitralux

1

2

[3] Trestle
CNC-cut plywood as a shadow of a
regency-style turned leg
Client: Ligne Roset

3

Nendo
Oki Sato
Hanabi
"The heat of the bulb makes this shape-
memory alloy lamp 'bloom' whenever the light
is turned on. 'Hanabi' is the Japanese word
for 'fireworks', or literally: 'flower + fire'."
prototype

Viable London
Charles Trevelyan
Harper

laser-cut steel table lamp with acrylic core

Ineke Hans
Forest for the Trees
Client: Lensvelt

Patricia Urquiola
Antibodi Chaise Longue
Client: Moroso

Tord Boontje
Icarus Light
Client: Artecnica

Sailor: "Hey, my snakeskin jacket... Thanks, baby...
Did I ever tell you that this here jacket for me is a symbol of
my individuality and my belief in personal freedom?"

Nicolas Cage in "Wild at Heart"

Customising is a way of giving individuality and uniqueness to everyday objects. It tends to be low-budget by definition — an adaptation of the found and available that prolongs, extends, enhances or alters their function.

The realm of the self-built, one-off always tended to belong to eccentrics, outsiders and hobby enthusiasts. One thinks of standard suburban gardens mutated through years of dedicated effort into fairy-tale gnome-lands decorated with myriads of trinkets and trash. Or beachcombers' huts bejewelled with flotsam, plastic bottles and limbs of dolls strung up between shells, stones and sand-smoothed wood. Auto enthusiasts soup up standard models of cars or motorbikes and tune them beyond recognition with spoilers and stripes, blinking lights and chrome detailing. People also customise their own bodies with tattoos and piercings, illustrating themselves with mythic beasts, Maori patterns, chunks of metal and the names of their loved ones. The hankering for individuality in our increasingly homogeneous global culture is as unquenchable as it ever was. Using decoration to mark ownership, a sense of status or difference is a human trait that has accompanied us since we were troglodytes.

We can customise our possessions, ourselves, our objects, our real and virtual spaces in a variety of ways. Generally we think of customisation by addition, as in the examples above, where the generic or ordinary is 'improved' in some way, primarily by decoration or adornment. The art of customising objects in our immediate personal vicinity by extending and embellishing given norms has entered the fashion mainstream of late in the form of a rediscovery of decoration. Embroidered and painted patterns and decorative elements began spreading across jeans, jackets and T-shirts and have continued onto bags, soft furnishings, through to furniture, light fittings, walls and floors.

This superficial form of decoration — a sort of neo-art nouveau — as addition or cutting out of elaborate pattern forms evolving from graphics, illustration, graffiti and tattoos is, thanks to current technology, readily adaptable to mass production and has therefore rapidly become a popular form of faux customisation. It gives the initial effect of individuality and the appearance of painstaking 'handcraft'. Also, by mixing a variety of decorative styles from folkloric to calligraphic this decoration lends an eclectic aesthetic to the final effect away from the spare modernist aesthetic that has dominated contemporary design for so long. When the Dutch designer

Tord Boontje introduced his Wednesday series of lacy flowered patterns as lampshades and furniture, he used new industrial processes to create patterns and objects and bring what he calls a new "sensual quality" to objects that could previously only be attained through very labour-intensive processes such as embroidery. There is some similarity here with the thinking behind the Arts and Crafts movement, but instead of a Luddite rejection of industrial processes, technology is now being embraced as a facilitator of decorative freedom.

Another reflection of the current vogue for dressing up the drab is the new meaning of the verb 'to pimp', made popular by the MTV series Pimp My Ride. This term is now used to signify the act of giving a flashy, eye-catching and unique appearance to something. Therefore, 'pimping' an object by giving it a makeover along the lines of customising a car is another example of customising in this category.

There is a form of customisation that arises out of necessity, such as sewing a patch onto an old pair of jeans, darning a sock, or mending a rip in the upholstery. An article of clothing or object is then altered in a practical way as a means of extending its useful life. Repairing objects tends to be frowned upon in our high-turnover, consumer-oriented world: when something is broken or worn out, you are supposed to throw it away and buy a new one. The US-based designer Jason Miller pays homage to thrifty virtues with his Duct Tape Lounge Chair where he 'mends' an armchair with strips of what appears to be industrial adhesive tape but in fact turns out to be strips of leather, thus incorporating a repair element into the initial design concept. "Don't denigrate duct tape," he says, "think of it as a badge of honour. It is a little piece of humanity. It is not something we should hide. It should not be banished. After all it's there because of us... And besides, maybe by fixing the chair before it is broken, it won't need to be fixed later."

Customisation through recycling is an extension of this thrift principle, although there is often as much statement involved as necessity these days: why make more new things when we can re-use these perfectly good old ones? Not because we have to but because we can choose to. Designer Karen Ryan scavenges rubbish containers, car boot sales and junk yards to find the material for what she calls her "Custom Made Furniture". Her throne-like chairs are amalgamations of dissected and reconfigured junk furniture inspired by her disgust at what she calls the "continuous waste in the pursuit of fashionable interiors". "I find it hard to watch the news and then consider the design of yet another superfluous object," she says, "So I make [things] from what others perceive as ugly and unwanted."

Many designers are now rediscovering the value of 'old' furniture. Either by learning to cherish a sense of history, tradition or narrative within older objects – the heirloom aspect – or with a sense of nostalgia for the ornate bourgeois homeliness of premodernist forms. The sculptor Ruth Claxton reconfigures and alters pre-existing domestic objects in a bid to question how we perceive or experience our modern world and reintroduce a sense of connection to the 'real' as against digital or virtual space which is "bookmarked not landmarked". Likewise, the Canadian artist Shary Boyle plays with the nostalgic element, but she explores the "tension between contemporary ideas and dated mediums" in a more critical way.

Her "sampled" porcelain sculptures, created using a painstaking technique known as lace-draping, reflect the transition of expensive hand-made porcelain figurines from the elitist "masculine" aristocratic preserve to a popular 20th century female hobby craft in the US and Canada. They are, for her, part of the tradition of New World artists: "Sampling, de-constructing, borrowing and reconfiguring your history. Like the expert recyclers we are."

Finally, there is a form of customisation through acts of subversion or appropriation where particularly symbolic forms or labels are 'altered' to change the message or meaning that was carried within the original. This is similar in thinking to the anti-globalism/anti-consumerism approach of customisation through recycling but is far more politically motivated as part of the anti-branding backlash exemplified in Naomi Klein's definitive 1999 book No Logo and practised by groups such as Adbusters or Reclaim the Streets. Maarten Baas' Smoke project – where he torches familiar and iconic furniture items often from well-known designers such as Charles Rennie Mackintosh's 'Hill House Chair 1' or Ettore Sottsass' 'Carlton' room divider and chars them black but not quite beyond recognition – may not seem (or be intended) to be a subversive statement, but could definitely be viewed as a collection of destructive or subversive acts of alteration that highlight our often obsessive veneration of certain furniture items or 'labels'.

Moa Jantze
Rocking Chair 2,
Red Chair, South Swedish Chair

Antoine+Manuel
Possession Chest of Drawers
silkscreen on black lacquer prototype
Client: Lafayette Maison

41

Studio Bility
Guðrún Lilja Gunnlaugsdóttir
<u>Visual Inner Structure</u>
felted wool and second-hand chairs

Raw Nerve
<u>Life Is Suite</u>
customised prototype sofa, one-off bespoke
design solution

42

Ryan Frank
<u>Hackney Shelf</u>
mobile shelving unit
"White boards are displayed at various points around East London attracting a variety of illicit activities. Once the boards have 'matured' they are removed and transformed into contemporary shelving units."

Duct Tape Lounge Chairs
upholstered chair with duct tape recreated in leather
"Don't denigrate duct tape, think of it as a badge of honor. It is a little piece of humanity. It is not something we should hide. It should not be banished. After all, it's there because of us. And besides, maybe by fixing the chair before it is broken, it won't need to be fixed later."

Jason Miller Studio
Mismatch Chair
"Notes for the upholsterer: It shouldn't take 7 yards of fabric to cover this chair. It's not that big. I bought 3 yards. Please make it work. I don't care if the pattern lines up. It's not important. If you run out, finish it with some remnants. Mismatch Chairs are chairs upholstered in the wrong way. Patterns don't line up. Prints are upside down. They may even have several different fabrics. Whatever."

44

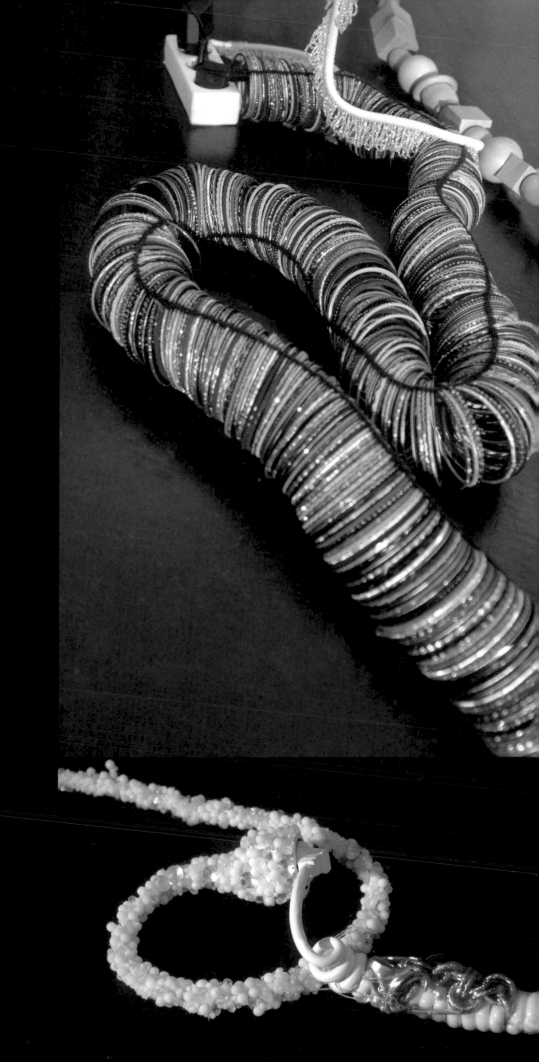

BLESS
Desiree Heiss + Ines Kaag
Cable Jewellery

Hrafnkell Birgisson

"Discarded players: radios, record players, tape recorders and CD players are reanimated with custom-recorded music tracks from various artists. The formal appearance of the chassis is kept but also implies the artist's appearance. A serially produced item is individualised and personified. Musician and music player are reconfigured."

[1] Una S
Client: Una Sveinbjarnardóttir
[2] Masha Grella
Client: Masha Grella
[3] Peaches
Client: Peaches
[4] Egill S
Client: Egill Sæbjörnsson

46

Robert Stadler
Culture Populaire
Fondation Cartier pour l'Art Contemporain

5.5 Designers
Galeries Lafayette VO Biche
Client: Galeries Lafayette VO

Johannes Carlström
Lumberlamps
prototypes

Bertjan Pot
<u>Old Fruits/Tops and Bottoms</u>
lamps made from the dried skins of squashes

Committee
Clare + Harry Richardson
'Crash' Kebab Lamp, 'Big Brother' Kebab Lamp,
'Mountain Rescue' Kebab Lamp,
'Sleep' Kebab Lamp

52

1

2

3

4

5

Shary Boyle
1–4 Untitled Figures
Collection: National Gallery of Canada.
53   5 Ouroboros

Ruth Claxton
"I thought I was the audience and then
I looked at you"
sculpture series, various media

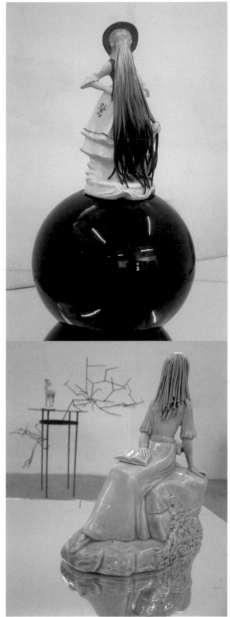

Ruth Claxton
A Place of Rainbows
sculpture series, various media

–opposite–
"It doesn't matter who you know 'cos this is real life"
various media

56

&made
Toby Hadden + Dave Cameron
Lost & Found' Series

–opposite–
Fulguro
Le Zinéma Interior
one-off originals for an independent cinema
interior in Lausanne
Client: Le Zinéma

5.5 Designers
<u>Reanim Furniture</u>
"How to accord a second life to a product?
This new discipline deals with communal
objects, many of which are to be found on
rubbish tips, on the streets, in homes or left
unsold and stocked in quantity at industrial
sites. The idea is neither restoration (return
them to their original form), nor to change
their intrinsic use (change their function),
but to give them a new life (by standardising
the intervention): simple actions that can be
reproduced by anyone or by a new industrial
process."
Client: Commissaires

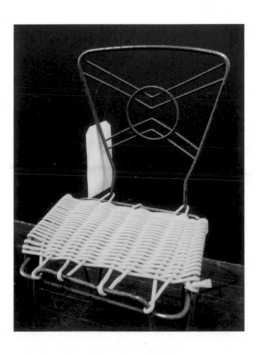

Karen Ryan
<u>Custom Made Furniture</u>
"Custom Made is as much about process as it is about product. I design and make furniture from unwanted and discarded furniture that I select from a scavenger's palette of fate. Strong memories of necessity and escapism make seeing unconventional beauty in the everyday essential. Sameness and familiarity are constantly reinvented into individuality. Compositions in function, form, colour and cultural references are considered in every detail. These elements play against each other in the creation of 'Custom Made', a unique furniture design and production process of the one-off that continuously evolves."

Karen Ryan
Custom Made Furniture

64

Rebecca Ahlstedt
<u>R-ocking Chair</u>
"R-use R-vitalize R-ocking chair: The re-use of
the global and low price plastic chair — can
you upgrade or alter the experience of the
object by giving it a new context? The design
is the principle: old object, new structure."
first prototype in collaboration with Källemo,
Sweden

Maarten Baas
<u>Where There's Smoke:</u>
<u>Dining Chair</u>
burned series piece 'Smoke'
Client: Moooi
<u>Campana Brothers' 2003 Favela Chair</u>
one-off burned furniture object
Client: Moss Gallery, NY

<u>Rietveld's 1918 Red and Blue Chair</u>
one-off burned furniture object
Client: Moss Gallery, NY
<u>Rietveld's 1934 Zig Zag Chair</u>
one-off burned furniture object
Client: Moss Gallery, NY

Dan Tobin Smith
Ash To Flash
'Broken Homes' photo shoot for Wallpaper*
magazine issue 72, October 2004. Smoke
chest of drawers + side table by Maarten
Baas, Porto vases by Gaetano Pesce. Shot
at Broomfield House, Palmers Green, London.
Built 1550, gutted by fire in 1984 and again
in 1994.
Interiors editor: Leila Latchin
Photo: Dan Tobin Smith

71

"...The case had its beginning
When I entered into the Art Exhibition.
To buy furniture that was my goal
In the newest, newest style.
There were chairs made out of human bodies
And even out of naked women,
There were books that were tables,
In the place of music stands there were octopuses,
Instead of lamps there were fire tongs,
Instead of footstools there were boa-constrictors,
Over the bookcases scrambled young scamps
And the glasses perched on iron poles.

And that was just exactly what I wanted.
It cost, of course, an ingot of gold,
But then as a reward
My entire apartment glittered in the newest style..."

Kory Towska

Design is about pattern, purpose and process: creative problem solving within given sets of parameters. We have already designed solutions for so many aspects of ourselves and our environment that each new problem rarely involves a truly novel solution. One would therefore expect designers to adapt existing answers within their particular discipline when approaching an everyday problem and occasionally look beyond into other fields of expertise should the need arise. But many designers now work less and less within traditional parameters. They may well still design chairs and tables, but they may, for example, design sounds, surfaces, time-based visuals or multimedia environments as well. They might work hands-on in wood for one project, hands-off with lasers and synthetic resins for another or in virtual space for a third.

A broadening of scope and dimension tends to bring a broadening of horizons with it, and it is therefore not surprising that as technologies improve and become more accessible, ever more designers are gripped by a new sense of Experimentierfreude — a delight in experimentation. They are taking materials, forms and objects out of standard contexts and remixing them; creating new conformations, new hybrids and new species of objects. The language being used is biotechnological as opposed to the biological vocabulary prominent at the turn of the 20th century. We are not talking about just echoing Mother Nature here — no Art Nouveau revival of organic growth, natural curves and imitations of life in crafted form as with the turn of the 20th century furniture of Henry van de Velde parodied by Kory Towska in the poem above — but about technological intervention, mutation of forms, grafting, splitting, interfaces, synthesis and the manipulation of archetypes.

When Dutch designer Jurgen Bey joined three bronze chair backs to a tree trunk and created the 'Tree Trunk Bench' in 1999 for Droog's Oranienbaum project, it marked the beginning of his series of experiments in transplanting furniture elements into each other to create new species of furniture. You could call him the Victor Frankenstein of furniture design were it not for the surprisingly peaceful and harmonious balance of his hybrid creations, where conflicting forms and materials such as junk store antiques and raw timber packing cases are fused together to create new functions and environments such as workspaces, sleeping cabins, bird-watching hides and playrooms.

Bey's pieces are mostly one-offs by definition — almost anti-design in their lack of relationship to 'product' — so too are the hybrid junk furniture pieces by French designers 5.5 or the mad chair mutants-turned-bookshelves by Maarten Baas, yet they don't only end up as artwork oddities in gallery spaces. There is considerable consumer and media interest for these pieces, proving that it is not just designers who feel a need for new furniture forms with a nostalgic twist.

Designers are revelling in their new-found, technology-fuelled creative freedom, but interestingly they are using this freedom to re-appropriate, sample and remix our relationship to the past. It seems that the further we travel into brave new worlds, the more we feel the need to carry with us homely vestiges of the familiar, like some kind of vernacular security blanket.

"Nowadays, the industry can do everything", says the young Spanish industrial designer Jaime Hayon; "The only future for design is to bet on pieces with emotion; those pieces that tell us about where we came from, our personalities." His first exhibition, called Mediterranean Digital Baroque, was an environment comprising illustrations, toys and ceramics in a bizarre blend of his own skateboard scene background, contemporary materials and a hint of historical twiddles. His first big commercial collection of bathroom furniture for Artquitect was an almost cartoon-like abstraction of Louis XIV in form, yet with a hi-tech feel. Hayon's 2005 Multileg cabinet for BD has parallels with Jurgen Bey's hybrids in that a simple, modular cabinet is fitted with a whole range of different ornate legs that the buyer can choose, mix and match to their taste — an ingenious method of adapting the one-off individuality of the new hybrid furniture style to the series product.

Like Bey, Hella Jongerius is another former Droog designer who is a master at tweaking tradition in her own way and for making the results commercially viable as well. She not only plays with mixing traditional and contemporary forms and materials but craft techniques as well, blending hi-tech and low-tech with assured élan in ceramic pieces for traditional porcelain companies such as Nymphenburg and Royal Tichelaar Makkum, as well as home furniture for Vitra. In so doing, she is bringing a sense of narrative and handcrafted individuality to contemporary domestic design that is reviving the notion of the home furniture object as a potential family heirloom rather than short-lived fashion object. But only time will tell whether her Polder sofas or Worker chairs get passed down through the generations or end up in the curiosity cabinet.

With their project Heritage in Progress, Swiss designers Big-game seek to place their objects in the "continuum of time" by adapting cultural references from "bourgeois culture" such as heavy tables, hard-to-clean light fittings and hunting trophies to contemporary mobile culture. They have kept the imagery and dispensed with the old reality by creating plywood flat-pack moose, stag and deer heads; lightweight trestles for budget tables with regency-style legs and gold-plated steel table lamps with fabric shades from building site spotlights.

Many designers have been remixing traditional porcelain and ceramics both with and without the blessing of the industry which is keen to throw off its antiquated image. Kate McBride has smashed and then reconstructed and augmented 18th century porcelain tea services into familiar yet alien forms; 5.5 Designers have undertaken a range of remixing studies of tableware for the French firm Bernardaud; Hella Jongerius has bound bronze handles with plastic ties to porcelain vases for Royal Tichelaar Makkum and Karen Ryan deconstructs decorative plate patterns into statements that have more affinity with conceptual art than willow pattern.

It is likely that in 15 or 20 years' time we will look back on many of these hybrids and transformed design objects as products of the dying throes of the bricolage style of postmodernism. As a brief nostalgic vogue; the last deep breath before stepping through the door marked 'future'. But there is a sense that our compulsion to retain a thread of tradition and form familiarity, souvenirs from our past, however abstracted, is something that will long withstand the caprices of fashion and progress.

Guido Ooms
<u>Lo-Res Chair</u>
"The digital world often forces trade-offs between two opposing preferences: speed and quality. When working with images, speed often translates to lower resolution, compressing elements to simplified shapes. During this process, it is the computer, compelled by necessity, that makes the decisions about what is taken out and what is left in. If we apply this bargain to existing products, we see that certain aspects of the product come to the forefront, while others recede."

Mareiße Gast
Broken Shelves

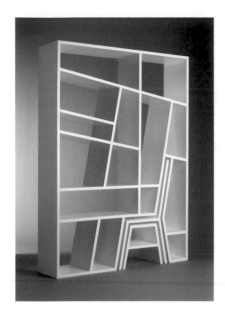

–above and opposite–
Viable London
Charles Trevelyan
Shelflife

Save Our Souls
Magdalena Nilsson + Johannes Carlström
Fuckin' Far From OK
shelf made of Valchromat
"The letters are extruded forming a shelf;
it's time to make a statement."

ding3000
Sven Rudolph, Carsten Schelling +
Ralf Webermann
<u>Odersoding</u>
modular shelf system

<u>Pimp My Billy: Billy Wilder</u>
"35 million units have been sold worldwide
of the Ikea shelf Billy – making it the world's
biggest seller when it comes to shelves.
Under the slogan 'Pimp my Billy', ding3000
have devoted their creativity to this classic
IKEA® piece."

Ünal & Böler Studio
Ömer Ünal + Alper Böler
Salkim Bookhanger

Jaime Hayon
Multi-Leg Cabinet
from the 'Showtime' series
Client: Bd Ediciones de Diseño

Jan Dijkstra
Dry Kitchenette

Scott Garcia
Embedded Meanings series
concrete, antique brass lamp, candelabra,
Victorian lace c.1860, one-off originals

Front Design
"Animal Thing"
Horse Lamp, Pig Tray + Rabbit Lamp
"Furniture to fall in love with at first sight,
or hate forever."
Client: Moooi

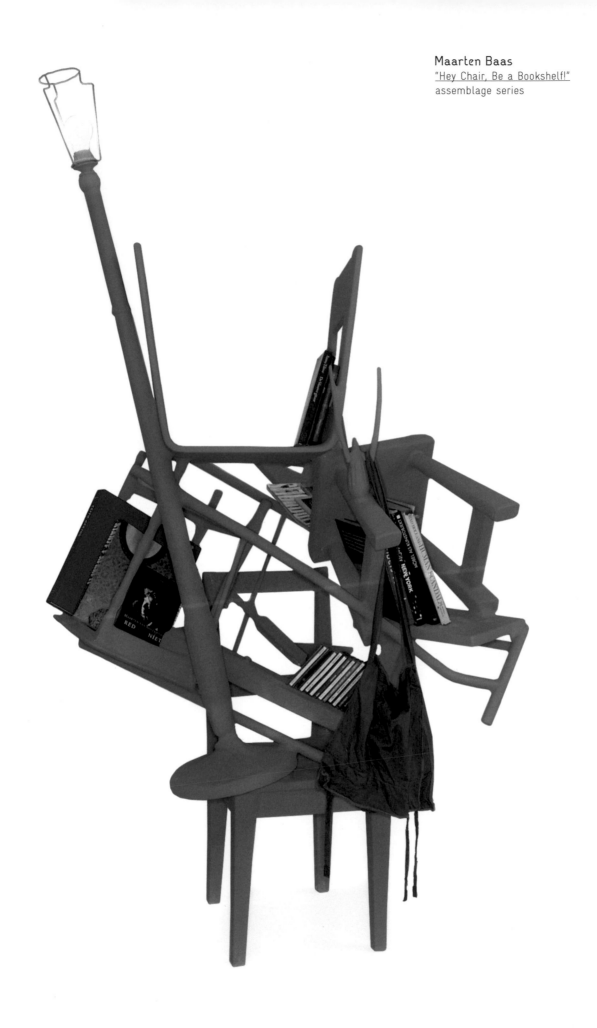

Maarten Baas

<u>Treasure Furniture: White Dining Chair</u>
made from furniture factory offcuts
"Since they reproduce their furniture, they
also reproduce the same kinds of waste.
That makes it possible for me to copy my
Treasure chair, as long as they keep on
reproducing the same waste."

Guido Ooms
Guido Ooms + Meinte van de Meulen
Rocker
"A universal attachment to turn almost any
four-legged chair into a real rockingchair."

Peter Traag
Rubber Chair 04
one-off original

Christine Centmayer
Object Gabriel
Object Andreas & Moritz

87

-opposite and above-

Hella JongeriusLab
Hella Jongerius
<u>Layers</u>
Details from "Five domestic 'interior fragments', mixed media 'assemblages', incorporating textiles, carved woodwork, cast bronze, and ceramics. Each is conceived as an intimate domestic moment, combining textile-based furnishings with the accompanying decorative objects they inspired, each becoming a complete work — or Gesamtwerk."
Client: Moss Gallery, New York

<u>Worker Chair</u>
Client: Vitra

-top and opposite-

Andreas Strauss

<u>Club 5 Interior</u>
Client: Wiener Festwochen, Vienna

<u>Tea + Coffee</u>
tuned second hand bedside tables with
synthetic leather, lacquer + gas stove
Client: Gabarage, Vienna

Tjep
Frank Tjepkema
<u>Table Accident</u>
"controlled collision of seven tables in
the conference room of an ad agency"
Client: Strawberry Frog, Amsterdam

Judith Seng
<u>Patches Tables</u>
prototypes

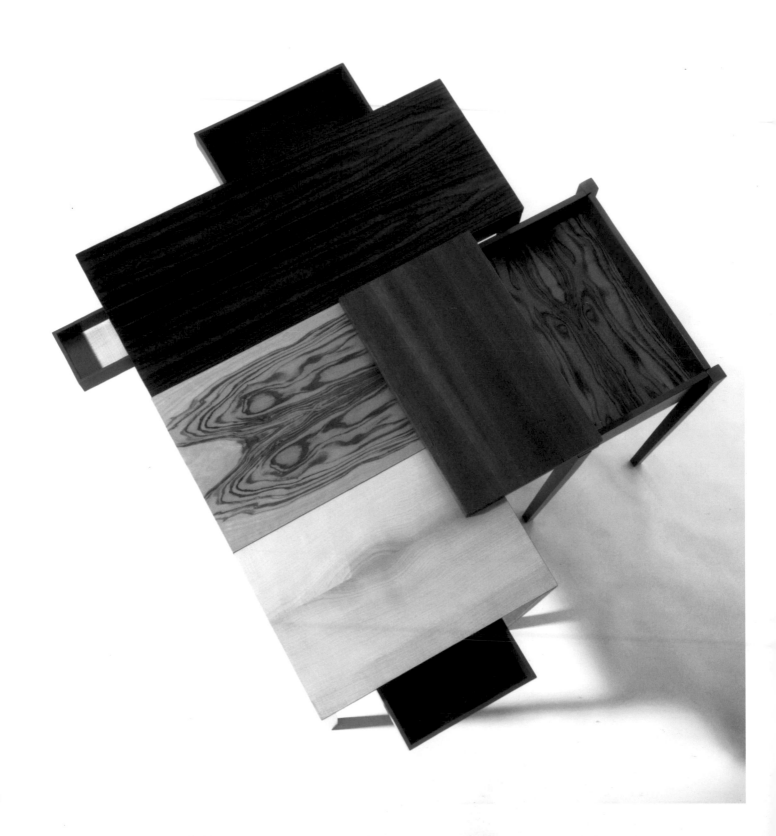

Super Robot
Tetsuya Hosokawa, Keiji Ashizawa,
Izumi Okayasu
Carpet Furniture

Liliana Ovalle
<u>Mugroso Sofa</u>
Royal College of Art graduation piece

El Ultimo Grito
Roberto Feo + Rosario Furtado
Tape Chair, Tape Sofa/Space
limited edition

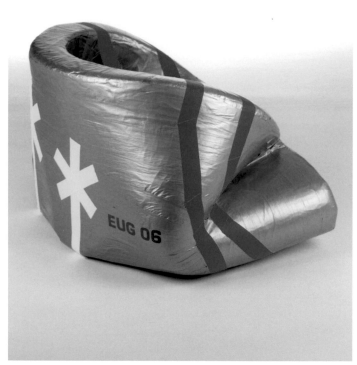

Jason Iftakhar
<u>Cardboard Bench</u>
Iftakhar developed a cutting tool that uses
standard supermarket packing machines to
turn old boxes into furniture

Liliana Ovalle
<u>Crash Bench</u>
Royal College of Art graduation piece

Jonathan Legge
A Wardrobe

Judith Seng
Hide + Show
wardrobe elements

Inga Sempé
Rangements (containers) Brosse
Client: Edra

Richard Shed
Magazine Reader Table
Client: Thorsten van Elten

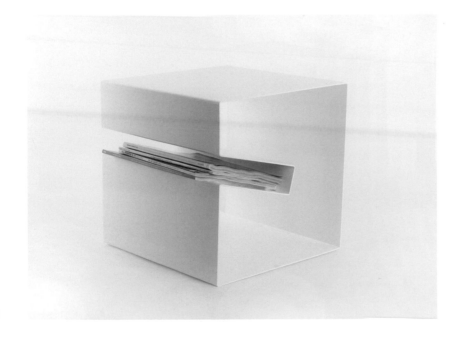

Jason Miller Studio
<u>Seconds</u>
"Products that are 'seconds' are products that
are not quite right. They are imperfect and
therefore of lesser value. But who made the
rules? Who says the decoration has to be
in the centre? Who says a flower can't grow
down? Who says a whole bird is better than
half a bird?"

–opposite–

Hate McBride
[1] <u>Mi-Sendup</u>
[2] <u>Your Krug is Sèvre'd</u>
Client: Moët Hennessy
[3] <u>Industrial Willow</u>

1

2

3

Guido Ooms

Guido Ooms + Davy Grosemans
<u>Dutch Delight</u>
"The sex toys designed by Ooms and
Grosemans are not just a joke. They refer to
the liberated sexual mentality of the Dutch
people. Making a dildo out of porcelain is
also a good example of using the right material for the right product. Glazed porcelain
has a soft and smooth skin which is hygenic
and pleasant to touch."
Client: EKWC

Karen Ryan
Second Hand
ornamental plates with original pattern
partially removed

Jason Miller Studio
<u>Superordinate Antler Lamps</u>
deer antlers cast in ceramic

WOKmedia
Julie Mathias + Michael Cross
<u>Flood Shelves</u>
Client: British Council

Viable London
Magnus Long
<u>Petit Fleur</u>

1

2

Viable London
Charles Trevelyan
[1] <u>Titanic</u>
[2] <u>Archipelago</u>

2

1

3

Demakersvan
Joep Verhoeven
How to Plant a Fence

Joris Laarman
Heatwave Radiator
re-inforced concrete, manufactured by
Droog Design and Jaga

"As a designer I feel like an explorer travelling the world out of curiosity, or being sent on a mission, investigating, asking questions and making connections. To come back with stories. Stories told with design because that is my language."

Jurgen Bey

We are evolving a new attitude to our domestic living spaces. Our home is no longer supposed to be regarded as a simple place of shelter and refuge but as an interface between us and the technological paraphernalia we need to make it function. Soon, we are told, our homes will have reactive skins instead of walls; ambient intelligence will control lighting, heat, humidity and the weekly food shop and we will furnish our residences with systems instead of objects.

In the early 20th century, the Bauhaus movement and the Deutscher Werkbund introduced one of the first notions of the 'modern home' by fusing traditional design and craft practices with industry and mass production. Le Corbusier also developed the concept of the Wohnmaschine — a vision of the home as an integrated labour-saving device; a modular unit for sleeping, washing, cooking and eating. We have had almost a century to get used to the idea of technology in our homes and to develop an appetite for design pertaining to that technology, but until recently, this has come to mean living in machines that are cluttered with, and aesthetically dominated by, the very technology that was meant to make them so sleek and efficient. The leisure age furnished us with no end of gadgets, from sound systems, beamers and remote controls to massaging armchairs and fridges with flat screens. As a result, our domestic landscapes are filled with wires and sockets and innumerable bulky, mismatched boxes with red stand-by lights.

But then everything started shrinking: our computers became laptops, our telecommunications went wireless, our sound systems became iPods, our cathode ray tubes have given way to slim, wall-mounted cinema displays and at long last we have loudspeakers that don't have to be the size of Manhattan tower blocks. Our materialistic statements are no longer about how much visible technology we possess but how little. The technology is being increasingly banished from view. We have space in our homes again. Space to fill with a different kind of clutter — space to create environments in. Our homes can still be labour-saving machines, offices, entertainment centres and whatever other functional devices we want them to be, but they can also be places of retreat and refuge to decorate as we want. When the technological apparatus of contemporary living no longer dominates spatially, this frees us up to play with our living areas and treat them more like theatrical or gallery spaces where we are the curators, the gallerists, the performers and the audience all rolled into one.

It is probably no coincidence that while our domestic technology has been shrinking, our interest in rampant patterns and ornate decoration has been growing. Since designers like Tord Boontje and Sounds of Silence created fairytale forest interiors of colour, light and pattern on trade stands for firms such as Moroso, Droog and Swarowski, the fashion for fantasy has skyrocketed. There is a sense of pop-up picture book worlds being brought to life in interiors as if people just couldn't wait to be rid of the shackles of modernist functionalism. Instead of glorifying the industrial aesthetic, designers are now pressing technology to the service of production techniques that create the impression of analogue or neo-organic environments — as far removed from the cogs and wheels (or chips and diodes) of our real world as possible.

Living environments do not just mean private dwellings of course. Public spaces, bars, clubs, hotels and even shops, galleries, offices, cars and trade fairs are all subject to this increased awareness of producing integrated ambient environments. Interactive installations are tending away from being a collection of touch screen interfaces and towards full immersion experiences where the temporary 'resident' can lose themselves in the designscape. These can range from environments that are sponsored or commissioned by manufacturers, retailers and labels to transmit the 'mood' they want to be associated with their products, through conceptual spaces created by designers to elaborate a wider context related to their designs, to fine art installations by artists.

Play environments are no longer the preserve of children. When we think of escape from reality and its mechanisms it is often into make-believe worlds with narratives and symbols that stem from our childhood. Our ideas of paradise tend to be retrospective, almost nostalgic views of places where it is allowed to touch, climb on and lose oneself in the scenery. Designing environments that fulfil those desires and allow adults to express their inner child by interacting with them is a far from childish preoccupation. As adults we have rediscovered play through our computers and playstations and it has become socially acceptable to indulge that need. It is only a logical step that more consideration be given to playful interiors and spaces now that we are banishing all that hard-edged, 'grown up' equipment. The soft 'settings' created by Anthony Kleinepier and TTTVo are good examples of play environments made with adults in mind, as are the tagged environments of El Ultimo Grito and Defyra's Domino environment. Outside spaces along the lines of tree houses, climbing frames and micro-architecture such as SMAQ's Bad and Andreas Strauss' Pipe Hotel are also becoming increasingly common.

Playing with parameters is another theme in contemporary environments. The photographer Dan Tobin Smith creates environments in his photography where scale and proportion are distorted in what at first glance seem to be perfectly normal interior settings. His staged imaginary spaces are completely wrong proportionally, yet completely believable in their theatricality. We have become used to and accept these new meta-realities readily, and again this is something that technology has facilitated for us through film and virtual realities. Fashion designers BLESS also play with scale and perception with their large format photographs of domestic interiors which they have printed on lengths of wallpaper. The effect of interiors within interiors in a home setting creates a disturbing disruption of our visual field and by superimposing one person's private space on another's the reality of that space is challenged.

So whilst we are in transit from our technologically dominated spaces to our technologically facilitated interfaces, we are at first learning to have fun in them. The relationship is still a long way from the symbiosis predicted by future forecasters, but it is starting to become conceivable that our Wohnmaschine is developing towards what we could call a Wohnorganismus as the technical apparatus becomes so complex and discrete that we are barely aware of its presence and its interfaces so smooth that they border on the intuitive. There could be a point in the not-too-distant future when we start to relate to our synthetic environments as 'living' organisms in their own right. Swiss artists Gerda Steiner & Jörg Lenzlinger explore the potential nature of this man-made environment-as-organism with their low-tech installations of junk and urea crystals that are synonymous with living, growing, vegetative organisms: They have created circulation and respiration systems that nourish crystal gardens and encourage them to sprout, flourish, decay and renew themselves in 24-hour cycles. The resulting brightly-coloured fantasy wonderlands are like synthetic rainforests — environments that are clearly initiated by human hand yet left to grow and change under their own impetus. If this is a glimpse of a possible future, then it is comforting to know that it is just as messy and cluttered with junk as the reality of everyday human environments we have always known.

Dan Tobin Smith
On a Grand Scale
'A Matter of Perspective' photo shoot for
Wallpaper* magazine issue 69, June 2004.
Up 7 foot by Gaetano Pesce, B&B Italia
edition, model tree from 4D Models, mini
pot from John Lewis, Vase 1 from the
Conran Shop, bonsai from Clifton Nurseries,
Rose from DZD, grand piano from Harrods,
Match lamp from Onedeko, Bowed lamp-
shade from Ann's, Fabric necklace by Anna
Osmer Andersen, chess piece from Big Game
Hunters, E305 vases from Oggetti
Interiors editor: Lyndsay Milne
Photo: Dan Tobin Smith

Dan Tobin Smith
The Long Stretch
'The Hard Stuff' photo shoot for Wallpaper*
magazine issue 88, May 2006. Henri I mirror
by Claudio Bitetti for Moco, Colombra chaise
longue by Cinzia Ruggeri, J16 cord from
VV Rouleaux, Log stool by Gervasoni, The
Lovers' rug by Fredrikson Stallard, Lunare
table by Brizzi, Parenti + Valliani for Dimos,
Carré lot no.1 concrete light by Nadine
Porter, Moses 4566 chair by Johan Celsing
for Gärsnäs, Housse de Chaise blanket by
Johanna Van Daalen for FR66.
Interiors editor: Leila Latchin
Photo: Dan Tobin Smith

120

Dan Tobin Smith
Delivering the Goods
'The Hard Stuff' photo shoot for Wallpaper*
magazine issue 88, May 2006. Ortofrutta
crates by Andrea Salvetti for Dilmos, Punto
mirrors by Claudio Bitetti for Moco, Kettle
from Studio Job, 1947 framed archivak print
by Bill Brandt from England and Co., Red
Rocky crystal heart by Baccarat, Frame +
Black Dot by Ron Gilad for Designfenzider.
Interiors editor: Leila Latchin
Photo: Dan Tobin Smith

Dan Tobin Smith
Having a Ball
'Strung Out' photo shoot for Wallpaper*
magazine issue 84, Dec/Jan 2006. Hands
coat hooks by Thelmont Hupton, Random
lights by Monkey Boys for Moooi, Less table
by Jean Nouvel for Molteni, Mummy chair
by Peter Traag for Edra, Strip light by Gitta
Gschwendtner + Fiona Davidson from Corian

Fulguro
Yves Fidalgo + Cédric Decroux
-opposite-
Waternetworks Exhibition
Client: The Lighthouse, Glasgow

-above and below-
Designer's Saturday Exhibition
Langenthal, Switzerland

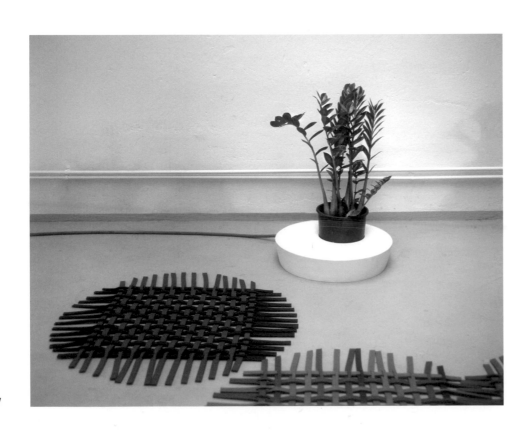

Jurgen Bey
<u>Vanishing Point 1</u>
ear-chairs, Dutch/Persian carpet, ceiling lamp
in exhibition for Klaus Englehorn 22,
Salone del Mobile, Milan

Andreas Strauss
Untitled
installation for Dialog III exhibition,
OK Centrum, Linz

BLESS
Desiree Heiss + Ines Kaag
N°29 Wallscape
Bless retrospective exhibition,
Boijmans Museum, Rotterdam

BLESS
Desiree Heiss + Ines Kaag
BLESSShop, Berlin
wallpaper with sleeping man: N°29 Wallscape:
Berlin, Mehringdamm, # 1C

-opposite-
BLESS Booklaunch
at Zucca Shop, Tokyo

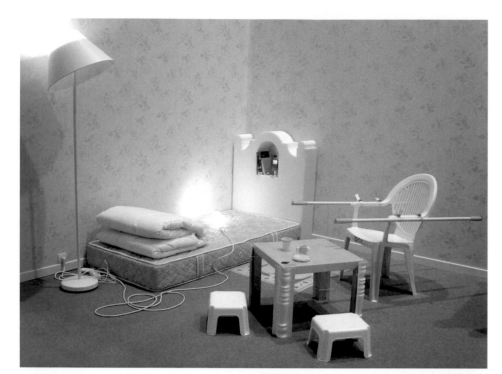

Untitled Carpet
Reanim, Milan

5.5 Designers
Objets Ordinaires: Supertable

134

Fulguro
Yves Fidalgo + Cédric Decroux
Furniture
prototype pieces of furniture for a private
architect's house

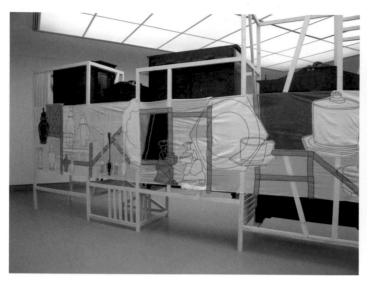

JongeriusLab
Hella Jongerius
Exhibition Design
exhibition around paintings from the Haagse
School
Client: Museum Singer Laren, Holland

Stefan Diez Industrial Design
Rosenthal Design Award 2004
exhibition space on the upper floor balcony
of the Pinakothek der Moderne in Munich
"Big balcony boxes including two slightly
inclined mirrors on the right and left side
of each box served to display the nominated
pieces. Whatever was placed in the boxes
was thus multiplied many times around the
gallery, so each project was transformed in
such a way that it filled the whole space the
moment someone was looking at it."
Client: Rosenthal

El Ultimo Grito
Roberto Feo + Rosario Furtado
<u>Primary Area</u>
table, stage, playground shelves, screen,
room divider
Client: West London Academy

Berthold Hörbelt + Wolfgang Winter
Swings
installation Tilburg, The Netherlands

Swingerclub Yokohama
installation Yokohama, Japan

Berthold Hörbelt + Wolfgang Winter
Museum mit Kisten
installation Museum für Moderne Kunst,
Frankfurt am Main, Germany

Berthold Hörbelt + Wolfgang Winter
Kastenhaus 560.10
installation at Kunsthalle Bremen, Germany
Kastenhaus 1666.14
installation Venice, Italy

Anyang Cratehouse – Dedicated to the Lost
(Pagoda)
installation Anyang, Korea

−opposite−
Feng Shui Basket Private Version
installation Frankfurt am Main, Germany

Tobias Reßberger
<u>Utterances of a quiet, sensitive, religious,</u>
<u>serious, progressive, young man, who</u>
<u>presumes from his deep inner conviction</u>
<u>that he is serving a good cause</u>
installation view, Galerie Bärbel Grässlin,
Frankfurt am Main

Tobias Reßberger
I Die Every Day, 1 Cor. 15,31
installation view, Palacio de Cristal, Museo
Nacional Centro de Arte Reina Sofia, Madrid

Tobias Reßberger
Geläut – bis ich's hör
installation view, Museum für Neue Kunst
MNK, Karlsruhe

Robert Stadler
Pools & Pouf!
leather elements installation,
Galerie Dominique Fiat, Paris
"These are parasites, whose presence raises
the issue of what a domestic world without
furniture would be like."
Courtesy: Klaus Engelhorn

Save Our Souls
Magdalena Nilsson + Johannes Carlström
Spill Glass Table with Metal Legs
"An unpleasant but seductive pool of oil
spreads over fragile ecological systems"
Drops Glass Lamp
"A black heavy drop of oil hangs above us
and spreads light and darkness."

Doshi Levien
"How are you?"
window installation
Client: Wellcome Trust

Doshi Levien

"How are you?"

window installation detail:
"Stethoscope that can hear your soul and
entices you to seek health through self-
questioning and reflection." Aluminium spun
shades, vacuum-formed heart, sculpted and
lacquered thorax.
Client: Wellcome Trust

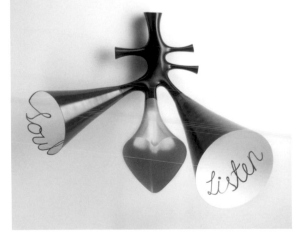

Robert Stadler
Frontalunterricht
Client: Espace Paul Ricard, Paris

148

Shigeru Uchida + Ikuyo Mitsuhashi
Moo Stools
installation Gallery le Bain, Tokyo,
upholstery by Sanae Awatsuji,
Meiko Kitahara + Kozue Hibino

Nina Braun
Nina Braun + Anneli Schütz
151   Bad Mood Cloud

El Ultimo Grito
Roberto Feo + Rosario Furtado
Tagged#6
Client: Stanley Picker Gallery, Kingston

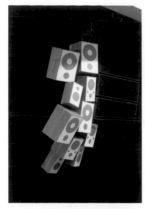

Fulguro
Yves Fidalgo, Cédric Decroux +
Geoffrey Cottenceau
Untitled
153   Client: Radio Suisse Romande

Robert Stadler
Alquimista + Têtes
Courtesy: Klaus Engelhorn, Vienna

Grande Tête
Courtesy: Klaus Engelhorn, Vienna

154

Peter Traag
LTD
Client: British Council

Anthony Kleinepier
Router "Salix Tristis"
outdoor seater at Erasmus University campus,
Rotterdam
Client: Erasmus University, Rotterdam +
Com.Wonen

Anthony Kleinepier
–above–
MU Setting
–below–
Router – Backbone
installation, Open Borders exhibition, Lille
Client: 24hliving

OnSite Studio
Sébastien Wierinck
On Site 02 — OS02 Bench

OnSite Studio
Sébastien Wierinck
On Site 05 — OS05 Bench
at La Friche la Belle de Mai, Marseille

Andreas Strauss
Dasparkhotel
minimal hospitality units, Ottensheim, Linz

160

Judith Seng
Veronika Becker, Heike Scheller + Judith Seng
Dressing: Clothing for Chairs

Andreas Strauss
Dasparkhotel
161   minimal hospitality units, Ottensheim, Linz

Tobias Reßberger
Rauminszenierungen
Schlosspark Wendlinghausen, Garten
Landschaft Ost-Westfalen Lippe

Moritz Eyoß Schmid
Nestwerk
shelter prototype

sixixis
Rolling House
"A piece of rolling sculpture made for children. It can be occupied, climbed on and rolled about, and is fixed in place using child-proof legs. It was designed using mathematical formulas intimately linked to patterns in nature and the Golden Number. The inner layer is oak and the outer layer is ash."
Client: private

Jurgen Bey
BLOB (Binary Large Object)

These are computer-designed shapes of fluent architecture, built using the Blowing Structure Method (BSM) developed by SKOR (Foundation for Art and Public Space) with Prof. Beunkers + students from the faculty of Aviation and Outer Space of the TU Delft. The "BLOB" can function as a theatre, cinema, research centre and temporary exhibition space. It is an independently functioning vehicle, but it can also clip onto the university to create extra workspace or be rotated through various angles to vary the interior space.
Client: SKOR together with TU Eindhoven

Ineße Hans
Forest For The Trees
Client: Koning Willem II College, Tilburg

166

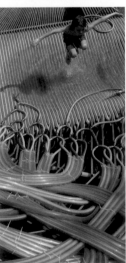

SMAQ

Sabine Müller + Andreas Quednau
<u>BAD (bath)</u>
infrastructural leisure equipment, Schloss
Solitude gardens, Stuttgart, Germany
"BAD is an architectural folly, a usable
sculpture based on a 1,000-metre long

garden hose, which can carry enough water
to fill a bathtub… The elastic hose forms the
surface of a screen that catches the sun, thus
heating the water in the hose."

Defyra
Anna Lang, Lena Thak Karlsson, Sanna
Haverinen + Anna Hjert
La Dolce Utopia e Tutti Frutti Della Defyra
installation at Designersblock, Milan: Defyra
lamp, ski stools and ski staff sideboard lamp   168

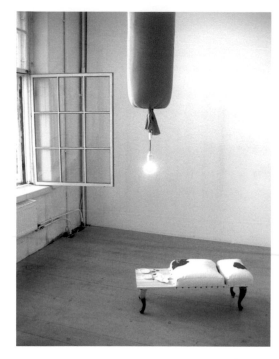

Defyra
Anna Lang, Lena Thak Karlsson, Sanna
Haverinen + Anna Hjert
<u>Domino</u>
installation, Studio 44, Stockholm

<u>Degree Show</u>
installation, Beckman's College of Design,
Stockholm

Anthony Kleinepier + TTTVo
Staged Authenticity #3:
Malicious Dumbo, Skull + Bones Seat,
Egg Chair (by TTTVo)
'Tingenes tilstand' – 'The State of Things'
exhibition, The National Museum of Art,
Architecture and Design, Oslo

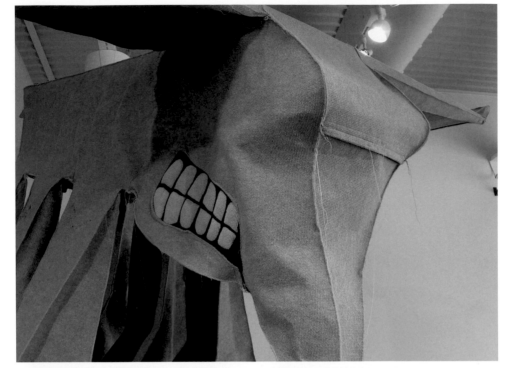

1 Anthony Kleinepier + TTTVo (stools)
Milan Setting
Client: Via Farini Gallery, Milan
2 Volcano Setting
installation, Art-U room Galeria Shibuyaku,
Tokyo

Sounds of Silence
Petra Eichler + Susanne Kessler
Sounds of Silence
light design: Herbert Cybulska, sound: Martin
Bott, video: Christl Pullmann
Client: Droog Design

−opposite−
Tord Boontje
Winter Wonderland
Client: Swarovski Crystal Gallery, Innsbruck

–above and opposite–

Tord Boontje
<u>Happy Ever After</u>
Client: Moroso

<u>Petit Jardin</u>
laser-cut steel, zinc and white powder coating

5.5 Designers
Balencoir Napoleon
Client: Galeries Lafayette VO

Gerda Steiner & Jörg Lenzlinger
Fuente de la Juventud
installation, 1st Seville Bienniale, Spain

−opposite−
s'Oberstübli
installation in a box for five people to stick
their heads in, Kunstraum Walcheturm, Zurich

Gerda Steiner & Jörg Lenzlinger
Le Méta Jardin
installation, la Maison Rouge, Paris

Gerda Steiner & Jörg Lenzlinger
<u>Seelenwärmer</u>
installation Stiftsbibliothek St. Gallen,
Switzerland

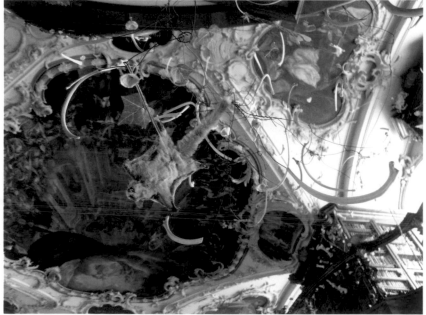

179

"Almost anything that can be drawn on a computer can be manufactured as well. The data set of the design has become the basis for production."

Gerhard Seltmann + Werner Lippert

Fashions fluctuate between the glossy and superficial and the carbuncles of gritty realism. We may admire perfect curves and super-smooth surfaces, but we also love to see how things tick and what holds them together — context, both internal and external fosters identification and a relationship to objects.

There is a certain satisfaction to be gained from being involved in the creation process of one's own furniture too. It was a stroke of genius on the part of IKEA to exploit the concept of flat-pack, self-assembly furniture. Not just because it saves production, storage and transport costs, but because for the customer it turns a cheap, anonymous, mass-produced item into something they can be involved with. The struggle with the instructions, the frustration and effort expended in putting together a wardrobe, table or bookshelf add a perception of individuality and history for the owner/assembler to an object that is ostensibly just the same as a million others in a million other households. Building a piece of furniture yourself, even at a superficial or almost symbolic level, makes it unique — it makes it yours. Some designers such as Form Us With Love, Fulguro, Ronan Kadushin and Super Robot have taken this self-assembly aspect and incorporated it as an integral feature into their furniture designs. Whether by presenting products as flat-pack items for the consumer to buy and build at home, or by incorporating the model or prototype aesthetic into the finished product, which then retains a certain temporary or unfinished quality.

Likewise, by witnessing the development of a high-end luxury item in the designer's workshop or the factory, you are seeing the diamond in the rough: away from the top model environment on perfectly lit tradeshow stands, a behind-the-scenes view also gives objects context and somehow makes them more desirable. This is something that the German car manufacturing industry has started to pick up on in recent years.

Henn architects' 2002 Dresden factory for Volkswagen's top-of-the-range limousine, the Phaeton, involves customers in the manufacturing process and the creation of their own individual product. Called the 'Crystal Factory', this transparent temple is where buyers can witness the creation of their very own vehicle, which is built mostly by hand in pristine conditions on oak parquet floors. Customers can spend three days at the factory being cosseted by their VW 'personal manager', who helps them through lacquer tones and seat leather swatches as well as organising opera and gallery visits whilst their new automated status symbol is put together by a team of craftsmen.

Designers are also exposing their design processes and making them more and more transparent. When a designer reveals the process behind one of his or her creations, they are demystifying it, making it accessible, more user-friendly in a way — but they also make it more naked and vulnerable. However, since plagiarism is also a rampant and almost accepted feature of the Knowledge Economy, there seems less reason to hide and more reason to acknowledge the enormous amount of work that goes on behind the scenes to bring a product to the public as well as to generate a greater intimacy with the finished product. Ronan and Erwan Bouroullec, for example, or Stefan Diez both have images of prototypes and experimental work on their websites. In this way, they highlight their creative thought processes and identity themselves with the process of their designs — beyond the distant finished pieces that end up in production with various manufacturers.

Back at the other end of the scale, the industrial is becoming more personal in another way: Technology is increasingly allowing designers to reduce the steps between the design and production processes, either through the increase in smaller, affordable and more refined mechanised tools, or through increasingly sophisticated 3-D computer software that allows the designer to develop a new product entirely virtually and then hand it on in data format to a machine to build it for them. One of the most exciting applied technological innovations in the past 10 years to have an effect on 3-D design is 'rapid prototyping' or RP. This is a collection of processes including stereolithography, selective laser sintering and fused deposition modelling that create highly accurate prototypes directly from CAD drawings, thus removing the need for casting, hand modelling or moulds in between. "There are no traditional design tools used whatsoever in the process", says Naomi Kaempfer, art director at .MGX Materialise, one of the pioneering companies working in RP design; "Everything comes from the 3-D software." Rapid prototyping not only makes incredibly accurate prototype objects, but also enables levels of three-dimensional complexity that were previously prohibitive. Here design is stripped down to the maths — a collection of algorithms made solid. Kaempfer again: "The .MGX designers... combine software packages and script their own tools to create unique and stupefying shapes. They twist our double-folded reality once more. With our rapid digital manufacturing techniques, we then turn these shapes into reality".

The basic principle of RP, in the case of stereolithography for example, is that a designer creates a 3-D file on their computer which is then sent to what is essentially a 3-D printer. The printer fires lasers into a container that slowly fills with fine layers of photosensitive epoxy resin dust and fuses or polymerises particles together in precisely defined volumes. When complete ('rapid' is something of a misnomer here — large objects such as chairs can take many hours to make), the excess powder is cleaned away with jets of air from the hardened resin object which emerges pristine from the dust like some precious archaeological artefact — or a do-it-yourself, high-speed fossil.

One of the enormous advantages of these techniques is that designers are no longer limited by the negative space problems involved in using

moulds and are suddenly liberated into a shape world that was previously the exclusive domain of Mother Nature alone. Therefore it is not surprising that many of the early forms of this technique, which is still in comparative infancy, are derived from natural structures such as skeletal structures, shells, corals and flowers — although more recent pieces from designers such as Assua Assuach and Patrick Jouin are achieving forms that truly seem to break new ground. An increasing number of designers in collaboration with companies such as .MGX, Freedom of Creation, Industreal and EOS, as well as government-supported institutions such as Met Works in the UK, are experimenting with rapid prototyping techniques and taking them from the niche area of prototypes for the automotive, medical and plastics industries into the high-end design market. It seems that once bitten by the bug of RP, many find it hard to even consider returning to the limitations of older and more traditional techniques. With their 2005 mission statement, "form follows formula", .MGX may just have coined the phrase that will define our shape world in the 21st century.

Super Robot

Tetsuya Hosokawa, Keiji Ashizawa +
Izumi Okayasu
<u>Flat Packing System</u>
laser-cut, 1.6 mm thick, standard sheet steel
folded along a "live hinge" perforated line
and strengthened using rivets and patches
"The perforated sheet of steel is a fun-to-see
object in itself. One would enjoy its ornamental quality even before it is transformed
into a product. What we have found in FPS is a
process of design which begins by scrutinising
the properties of a material, and the technology that is required to take advantage of such
properties. We are expecting this process
to result in many different adaptations."

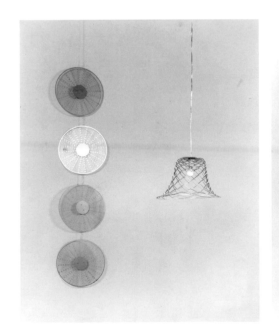

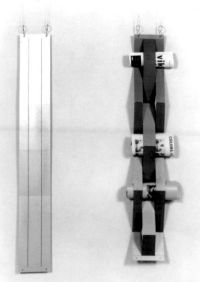

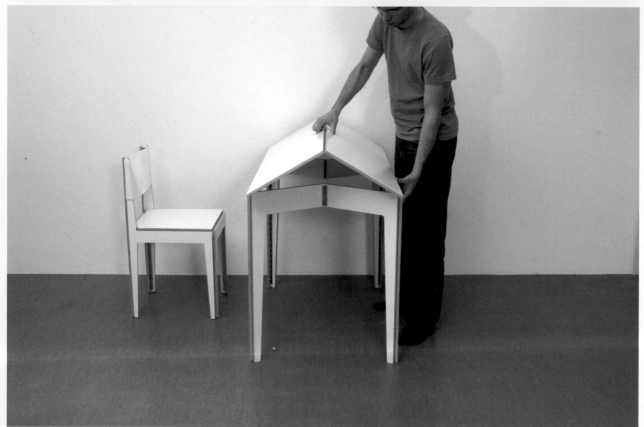

Fulguro
Yves Fidalgo + Cédric Decroux
Servier Boys
research project/prototype

Form Us with Love
Petrus Palmér, John Löfgren + Jonas Pettersson
<u>Group of Trees</u>
A flexible and sound-absorbing room divider for public spaces, adjustable in both width and height. Mobile modules made of pressed polyester felt are easily attached to one another without tools via a pin-fitting device. A cylinder moulded into the aluminium base allows a 360° rotation so that the user can choose the level of visual blocking.
Client: Materia

Ronen Hadushin
Eclipse
Client: Open Design

Ananda
prototype

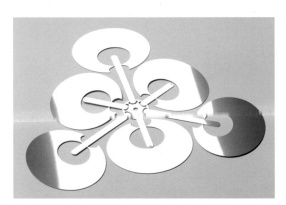
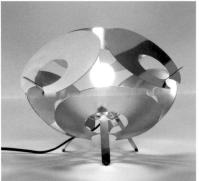

Ineße Hans
Credit Card Cutlery
Client: Cooper Hewitt National Design Museum

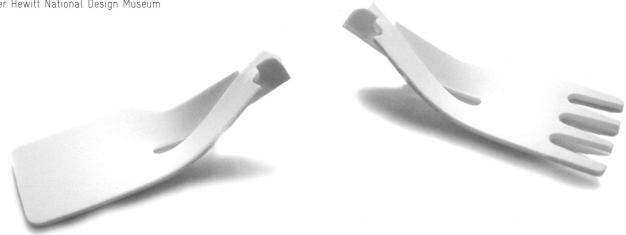

Ronen Kadushin
Low Square Dance
prototype

Ronen Kadushin
Flat Knot, Round Square Dance
Client: Open Design

Form Us with Love
Bendable Interior Objects (B.I.O.)

B.I.O. Office Kit (pen holder, letter rack + business card holder), B.I.O. Coat Hanger, B.I.O. Stool.

"B.I.O. is a futuristic vision: a concept built around the flat and slimmed production processes of today, where terms like packaging, assembly, transportation and environment are hot topics. B.I.O is laser-cut in recyclable aluminium and comes in the shape of a flat 'bag', easily carried home by the buyer. The user then snaps the objects out of the sheet metal and folds them into their intended shape by hand. By thinking B.I.O, we can save space, costs and the environment."

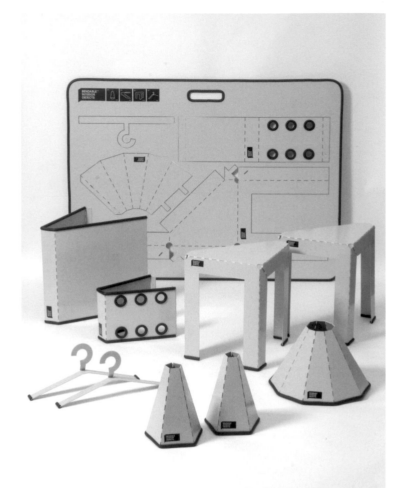

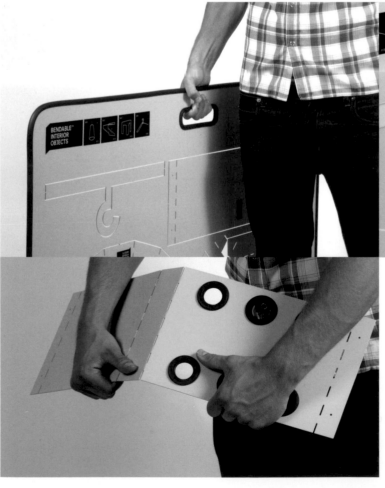

188

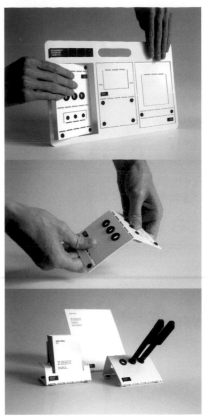

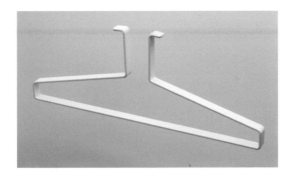

189

Big-game
Elric Petit, Augustin Scott de Martinville +
Grégoire Jeanmonod
<u>Folded Bench</u>, <u>Folded Table</u>
table for indoor/outdoor use made from a
single sheet of folded alucobond
made at Ecal, Lausanne

–opposite–
<u>Folded Lamp</u>
LED lamp series using origami-style folded
alucobond. The electricity runs through the
material.
made at Ecal, Lausanne

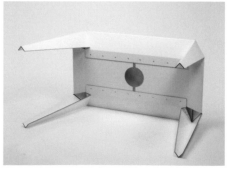

Patrick Jouin
SOLID C1 Chair, SOLID T1 Table
photopolymer liquid + solid stereolithography
technique
"The possibilities and advantages of an
industrial-scale tool that produces infinite
quantities of identical objects with maximum
simplicity and without additional costs are
clearly palpable. Furthermore, pieces previously impossible to fabricate with a mold
can now take form. This form is based upon
establishing a new approach to the creation
of the object. Thus, SOLID is about inventing
a process."
Edition: .MGX Materialise

Industreal
<u>Model Ideas</u>
exhibition, Milan 2005, showing rapid
prototyping work produced by the company
from the designs of 60 young international
designers

Industreal
various designers
'Dream'
rapid prototype technology exhibition

[1] Pierre Foulonneau
Déjà-Vu
[2] Stefano Citi
The Little Alchemist Set
[3] Frida Andersson + James Steiner
Smokes Like A Chimney
[4] Simone Simonelli
Bird's House

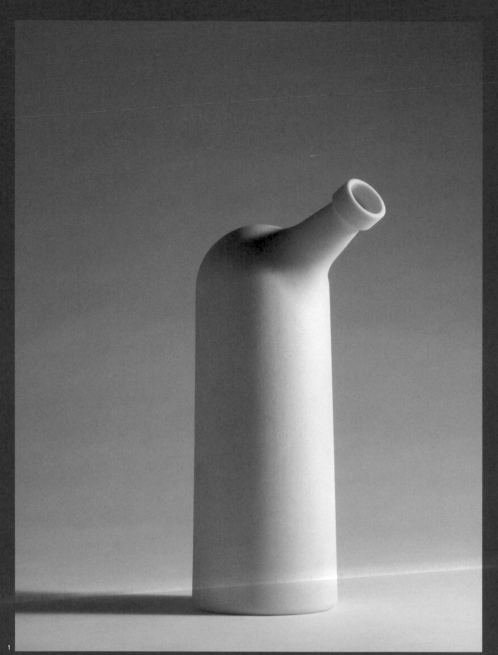

Industreal
Michael Radix + Céline Steelandt
<u>Programmatotem</u>
rapid prototype technology from the
'Model Ideas' exhibition
"Each element of the totem represents a
prugramming change of the machine that
manufactured it."

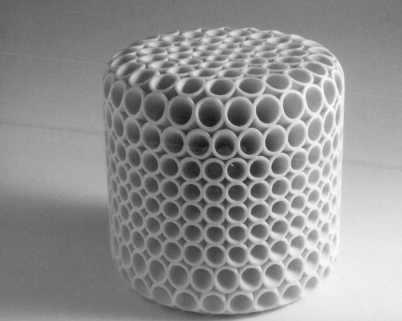

Richard H. Mills
<u>Lord, Blow The Moon Out Please</u>
rapid prototype technology from the
'In Dust We Trust' exhibition

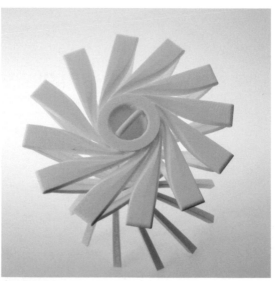

Patrick Jouin
<u>OneShot</u>
folding polyamide stool made by selective
laser sintering
Edition: Materialise .MGX

Materialise .MGX
Bathsheba Grossman
<u>Quin</u>
nylon + epoxy lamp made using selective
laser sintering technology

Freedom of Creation
Janne Kyttanen
<u>Dahlia</u>
laser sintered polyamide wall lamp

Freedom of Creation
Janne Kyttanen
<u>1597</u>
laser-sintered polyamide wall lamp

¹Jiri Evenhuis
<u>Venus</u>
laser-sintered polyamide wall lamps
²Janne Kyttanen
<u>377</u>
laser-sintered polyamide table lamps
"377 is based on the Fibonacci sequence of
numbers appearing in nature all around us.
[It is] inspired by the cone flower and the
growing pattern of its seeds."
³Janne Kyttanen
<u>Palm</u>
laser-sintered polyamide hanging lights

1

2

3

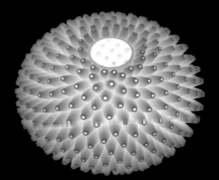

Freedom of Creation
Janne Kyttanen
Palm, Spin 10, 610
laser-sintered polyamide hanging light

–opposite–

Materialise .MGH
Bathsheba Grossman
Flame
nylon polyamide lamp made using selective
laser-sintering technology

204

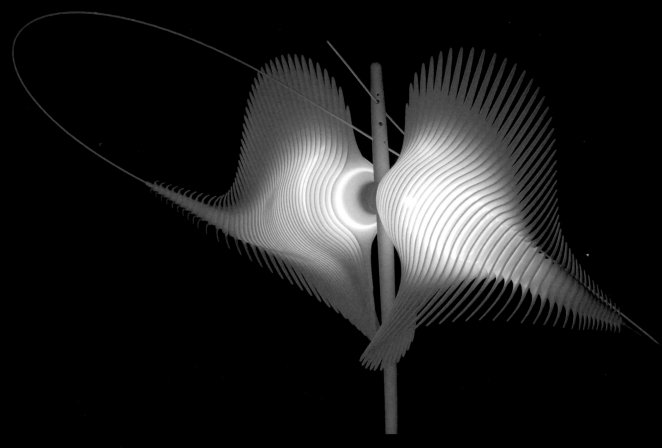

Materialise .MGX
Assa Ashuach
<u>OMI .mgx</u>
nylon polyamide lamp made using selective
laser sintering technology

Assa Ashuach
<u>FLY .mgx</u>
selective laser sintering prototype for
.MGX Materialise

206

Assa Ashuach
<u>Osteon Chair</u>,
<u>AI Stool</u>
selective laser sintering
Sponsors: EOS, Complex Matters,
Metropolitan Works + Autodesk

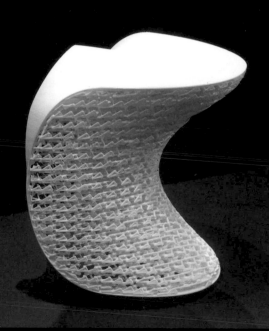

sixixis

Tom Raffield, Charlie Whinney, Chris Jarratt
<u>Chaise Longue No. 4</u>

UK-based sixixis work in wood and are committed to combining sustainable and traditional methods with new technology for their hand-crafted furniture. Three technological innovations developed by the designers form the basis of their furniture forms:

"The first is a new method of steam-bending wood developed by Tom... that enables us to twist and bend wood in any direction, on any plane. We can easily achieve any 2D or 3D bend you can imagine, accurately and cheaply, with a much higher success rate than using traditional techniques.

The second is a unique modular jig-system that enables us to accurately plot any curve in 3D space, transposed directly from a range of CAD packages including AutoCAD, 3D Studio Max and Solidworks.

The third is the unique sixixis grid shell system developed by Charlie. sixixis grid shells are built up in layers to create organic wooden structures of unparalleled strength and lightness. This technology grew from a desire to see wood as a tensile engineering material."

Studio Bility
Guðrún Lilja Gunnlaugsdóttir
<u>Flatpack Antiques</u>
plastic-covered wood series that incorporates
the illusion of woodcarving into modern furniture using new materials

Demakersvan
Jeroen Verhoeven
<u>Cinderella</u>

"Industrial production is a big source of inspiration. The big miracle of how some some industrial products come about is a wonderful phenomenon if you look at it closely: the high-tech machines are our hidden Cinderellas. We make them work in robot lines when they can be so much more. In the 'Cinderella' project, that thought is translated. To make the table we used a high-tech method as our new modern 'craft'.

Sketches of old furniture are put together in a computer, which translates them into a drawing that can only exist in a digital world. The table is CNC cut out on a three and partly five axes machine. It is made out of 57 layers of birch multiplex and is finished by hand. It is about attention and the possibility of making something unique with a machine that is normally used for mass production."

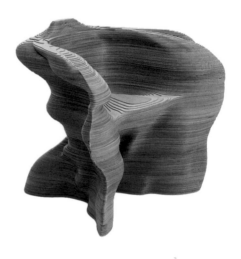

211

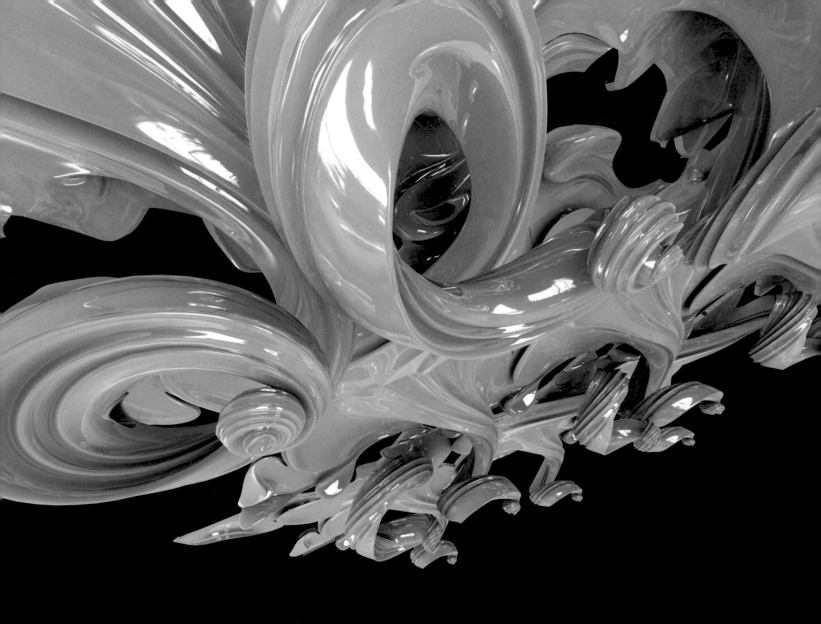

Evan Douglis Studio

<u>Helioscopes</u>

fibreglass travelling mediascape

"In the dream of recombinant technology and biologically mimetic surfaces for the future of architecture, Helioscopes represents an alternative model of production, seamlessly obedient to the processes of modern strategy. Situated somewhere between a search for topological indeterminacy and an oneiric vehicle of desire, this seemingly lifelike fleet of media-scape stalactites represents an entirely new synthetic ecology.

Originally commissioned by the FRAC Centre for the 2004 Archilab symposium and exhibition, Helioscopes as a marketing strategy is offered as a single module or in multiples suspended across an aerial terrain. Each of the helical tails contains a single vision orifice through which an endless itinerary of fantasy settings are available to the consumer with a propensity for consumption. Outfitted with the most recent advancements in membrane and information display technology, this new wired flesh serves to highlight the endless algorithms of difference found in the indeterminacy of everyday life."

Client: FRAC Centre, Orleans

213

Joris Laarman
<u>Bone Chair</u>
Single cast, polished aluminium chair made in a limited edition of 12, using a new CAD/cast technical ceramics mould method developed by Gravotech that is designed to take new RP-facilitated forms beyond the material limitations of rapid prototyping. Laarman consulted with a bioengineering specialist who had developed a dynamic digital tool to imitate bone growth: "Bones are extremely efficient since they are able to add material where strength is needed and also have the ability to take away material where it is not needed. The tool can be applied to any scale," says Laarman; "I used it as a high tech sculpting tool. The result has an almost historic elegance that is far more efficient than modern geometric shapes."
Client: Droog Design + Barry Friedman Gallery, NY

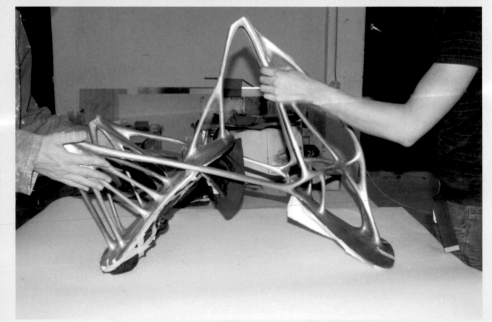

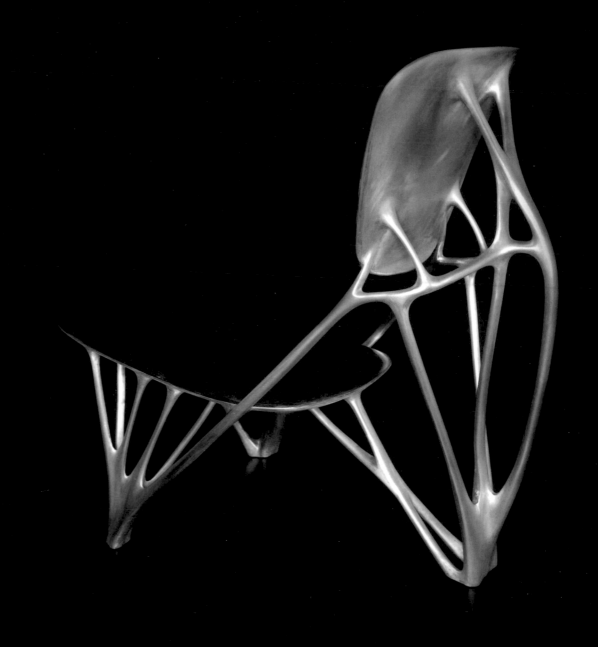

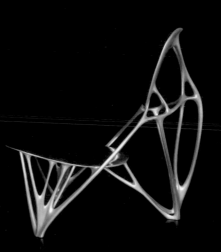

Stefan Diez Industrial Design
Stefan Diez
<u>Friday Chair</u>
prototypes
Client: Elmar Flötotto

Konstantin Grcic Industrial Design
Konstantin Grcic
Dummy Chair
polyurethane chair prototypes
Client: Moroso

Ronan + Erwan Bouroullec
The Tiles
compressed fabric and foam tesselating tiles
as wallcovering, prototypes
Client: Kvadrat

Slow Chair
research/prototype
Client: Vitra

Facett
conception/prototypes
Client: Ligne Roset

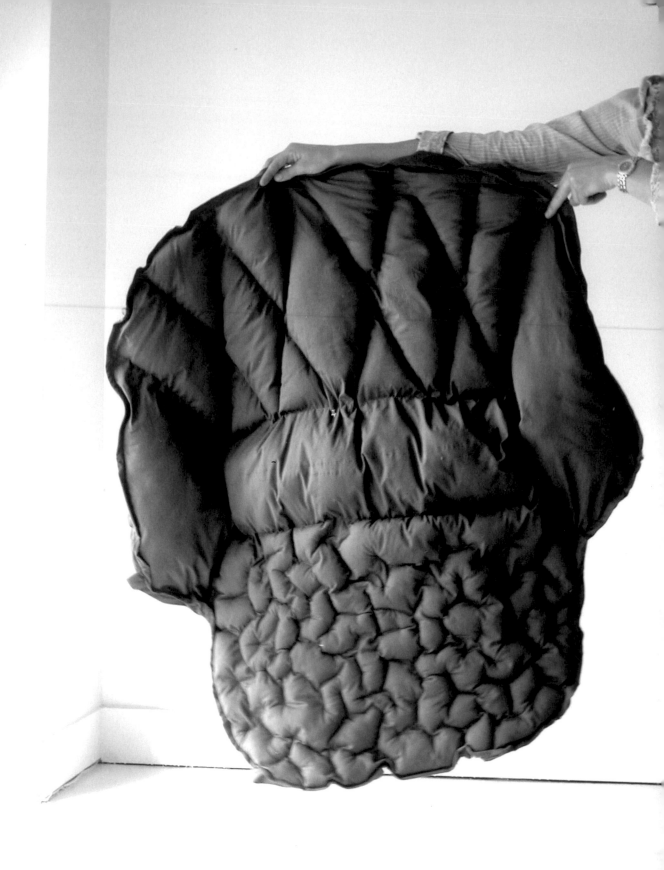

Ronan + Erwan Bouroullec
<u>Slow Chair</u>
research/prototype
Client: Vitra

Nendo
Oki Sato
<u>Polar</u>
"The size changes as the three side tables are
stacked or lined up together. When the tables
are stacked, the polarizing film inside the table
top makes flower patterns appear through
the clear glass surface. We named the tables
'polar' because of the polarizing film, and
because they look as though trapped in ice."
Client: Swedese

Front Design

<u>Sketch Furniture</u>

"Is it possible to let a first sketch become an object, to design directly onto space?"

The four FRONT members developed a method to materialise free hand sketches by combining two advanced techniques: Pen strokes made in the air were recorded using Motion Capture (a software usually used for film and computer game animation) and translated into 3D digital files; these are then materialised through Rapid Prototyping into real pieces of furniture.

Collaboration partners: Barry Friedman Ltd., Tokyo Wonder Site Aoyama + Crescent

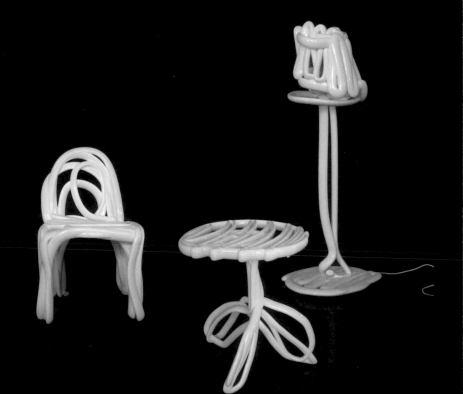

Evan Douglis Studio

REptile

In Japanese mythology, reptiles are considered both sacred and virtuous. Evan Douglis studio proposed a new mimetic 'animate-skin' surface, designed using animation software: "This was achieved by superimposing two independent meshes (pyramidal vs. smooth) within the animation software, fluctuating at different frequencies in order to create a variety of productive interference patterns. Through the use of controlled chance, an extensive menu of surface effects emerged offering an increase of options for the discerning eye. The changing scale and rotation of the matrix of pyramids work to redirect the light and shadow in such a way that a greater depth of field is perceived." Although the animate surface seems highly complex and visually active, it is in fact made of a modular system of mass-produced liquid plastic tiles finished with hi-gloss, red, car paint. The original master was CNC-milled out of renshape on a five-axis milling machine and then transferred into urethane moulds. Client: Haku Japanese Restaurant, NY

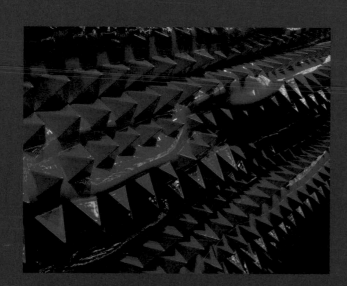

"In the next century, when art will be packaged as virtual reality software, realistic paintings will sell the way Shaker furniture does now. Shaker furniture will sell the way Van Gogh paintings do. And teddy bears owned by Elvis will come to auction only occasionally."

Brad Holland

In the world of fine art investment, design always tended to be viewed as art's inferior sibling; a wannabe art form with ideas above its station. But now, with one-off pieces of contemporary furniture fetching the kinds of prices at auction that we are more familiar with for traditional fine art, gallerists and collectors are looking to their Emins and their Eders and starting to wonder whether the addition of a Bouroullec or a Jongerius might not be a wise investment after all.

As recent auction sales and the rocketing success of the new Design Basel/Miami and Design Miami extensions to Art Basel and Art Miami fairs testify, buyers just can't seem to get enough of limited edition and one-off pieces by current celebrity designers such as Ron Arad, the Campana brothers or Marc Newson. Even architects, like the grand diva Zaha Hadid herself, are turning a hand to saleroom-sized objets. Whether this is a buyer backlash against the difficult-to-grasp and object-free realms that contemporary art has moved towards (concepts never were very easy to hang over the fireplace), or the latest step in the eternal quest for the next fresh thing, this increased interest is bringing design closer to fine art than it has been for centuries. It is design's connection to function that is making these objects more desirable. And it is a development that is making waves in both directions: even young fine artists these days are bringing craft into their studios and their work.

"What is happening to the market now is not too dissimilar to the situation around 1900", says Marcus Tremento, senior specialist in 20–21st century art design for the auctioneers Philips de Pury in New York; "The Paris Exposition threw everything together; ceramics, glass, furniture, painting, jewellery and so on." Tremento believes that elements that had become the domain of manufacture are now turning back to craft: "Design and Art used to be separate but now everything is in one place again and this is what dealers are finding so exciting."

In one respect a 'return to craft' means prototypes: even in the world of mass production, designers create prototypes, hand-crafted one-offs, experiments that are often produced at great expense and with great skill, testing new materials and forms, or perhaps just mapping out a thought or sketch in 3-D to see if it could work. Even Charles and Ray Eames' ubiquitous DCM chair had a prototype once. It was the first, unique, or at most one of a mere handful and therefore special and highly collectable. Sometimes a prototype stays just that and never goes into production. It remains just a thought, but it can be a thought of such beauty and balance that it transcends the original intention and becomes art.

There is now an emerging industry generating prototypes and limited edition design objects for a collector elite seduced by beautiful work and finishing, coupled with the exclusivity born of rarity. The British company Established & Sons is pioneering this new niche by successfully combining high-end craftsmanship and materials with a select stable of designers and the exclusive packaging of a gallery. Their first 'premier collection' was launched in 2005 and was quickly followed by a 'Limited Editions' selection, aimed specifically at museums and collectors, which includes Zaha Hadid's Aqua table and Future Systems' Chester sofa. Collector, dealer and gallerist Kenny Schacter of the Rove gallery in London has witnessed a flourishing interest in these limited editions and prototypes over the last couple of years and doesn't see it letting up: "The trend will be to continue a more thorough integration of contemporary art with new design. It is a matter of time before the highest regarded design ends up in art auctions achieving art prices."

According to Marcus Tremento, that time has already arrived. At a Philips design art sale in December 2005, a Zaha Hadid table, one of only three prototypes ever made, went for $296,000. "Or Marc Newson, for example, yes, he is an industrial designer licensed by Alessi, but he has also made heavily crafted objects like his Black Hole table that was intended to be a production piece, but only two or three were made. One of these sold at auction in Australia in 1997 for $5-6,000, now it is coming back up and is expected to achieve $100-150,000. That's a tenfold increase in value." Other recent sales include a 2003 Sushi Sofa prototype from Fernando and Humberto Campana, which sold at Philips for $84,000 and a pair of 1990 steel chairs by Scott Burton, which went for $198,000.
That is a lot of cash for furniture objects, but when you compare the prices to those of fine art pieces, says Tremento, they are still reasonable for iconic works. "If you are someone who can shell out $800,000 for a Damien Hirst, then buying an equally recognised and definitive design original for a tenth of the price is really very good value."

Peter Wesner is a member of the board of the international auditing firm KPMG in Frankfurt and an avid collector of contemporary design objects, especially those of Ron Arad. He collects for love rather than investment: "Crafstmanship fascinates me," he says, "and design that combines form with feasibility. My favourite TV chair is Ron Arad's Big Easy. People ask me how I can possibly watch TV in a steel chair, but it's comfortable! It works, that's what I admire about it." Wesner is a good example of this cross-over attitude to design object collecting. Most people would never dream of using their Rodin as a coat stand, but somehow sitting on your Arad is not yet really considered to be a sin. It is what it was made for after all. But now that the Arads are pushing five figure prices, this attitude may also be changing. "Some of Jasper Johns' pieces were also interactive when they were first exhibited, but if you touched them now, you would get arrested", notes Tremento.

But how much of this market boom is a result of hype? How do you distinguish the fad from the far-sighted? "Value is in the mind of the buyer," warns Kenny Schachter, "but if you aren't a connoisseur or haven't developed a notion of why you are doing something then you will err." Peter Wesner is wary of the hype and the prices. He believes there are many designers being lauded out there that won't stay the distance along with many unserious collectors: "There will always be a group of individuals that spend their money on design objects because they find it chic, for decoration, not for content or intention."

But for Tremento true quality just shines out and there can be no mistaking it when you see it: "We are in an age in which we have lost our perspective on what we want visually. We have become addicted to freshness. The Campanas' Sushi sofa is a perfect example; it is so much about enjoyment and pure craft. What makes it special is how different it is. It hits you in a certain way and changes something. You may say 'I've seen that a million times already' but in reality there is only one."

Ronan & Erwan Bouroullec
Galerie Kreo
Assemblage #4, Assemblage #2,
Assemblage #3
from the Assemblages collection 250, 150, 60,
edition limited to 8 + 2 artist's proofs +
2 prototypes, pieces numbered + signed
Client: Galerie Kreo

Established & Sons

<u>Milan Exhibition April 2006</u>

Established & Sons is a UK company launched in 2004 with the aim of bringing together a premier selection of British designers with British manufacturers (the Caparo Group) to create a new range of high-end furniture products. Through careful marketing and exhibitions at the Milan Salone, 100 % Design Tokyo and Design Miami/Basel, the company rapidly became a lifestyle media darling. Their Limited Editions range, billed as "spectacular renditions of unique and ambitious designs", is aimed specifically at wealthy collectors and cult status:

"Wildly covetable, supremely desirable, this collection of work has already enjoyed the attention of major international collectors, institutions and museums."

Zaña Hadid
Established & Sons
Black Aqua Table
limited edition
Client: Established & Sons

Future Systems
Established & Sons
Drift Bench
limited edition
Client: Established & Sons

Established & Sons
Drift Bench by Amanda Levete, Future
Systems, Zero-In Table & DLWP Chair by
BarberOsgerby
–opposite–
DLWP Chair by BarberOsgerby, The Crate
by Jasper Morrison + The Fold Lamp by
Alexander Taylor
Client: Established & Sons
Photo: Peter Guenzel

Philip Michael Wolfson
WallDance Console + Ripteal Shelves
limited edition (10 + 20), aluminium +
UV laminated, layered float glass
Client: Contrasts Gallery, China

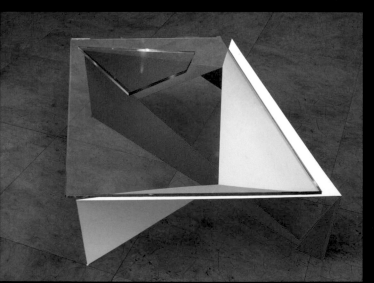

FloorDance Coffee Table
limited edition of 10, aluminium +
UV laminated, layered float glass
Client: Contrasts Gallery, China

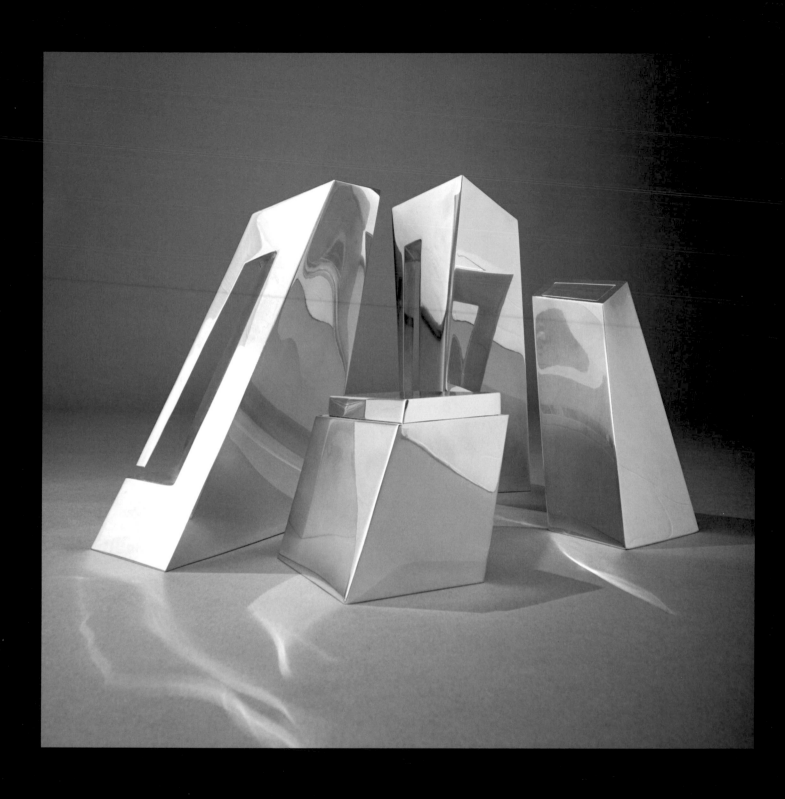

Zaña Hadid
designer's gallery//gabrielle ammann
Tea + Coffee Set
sterling silver

Satyendra Paßñalé
designer's gallery // gabrielle ammann
Flower Offering Chair
exclusive to designer's gallery // gabrielle
ammann

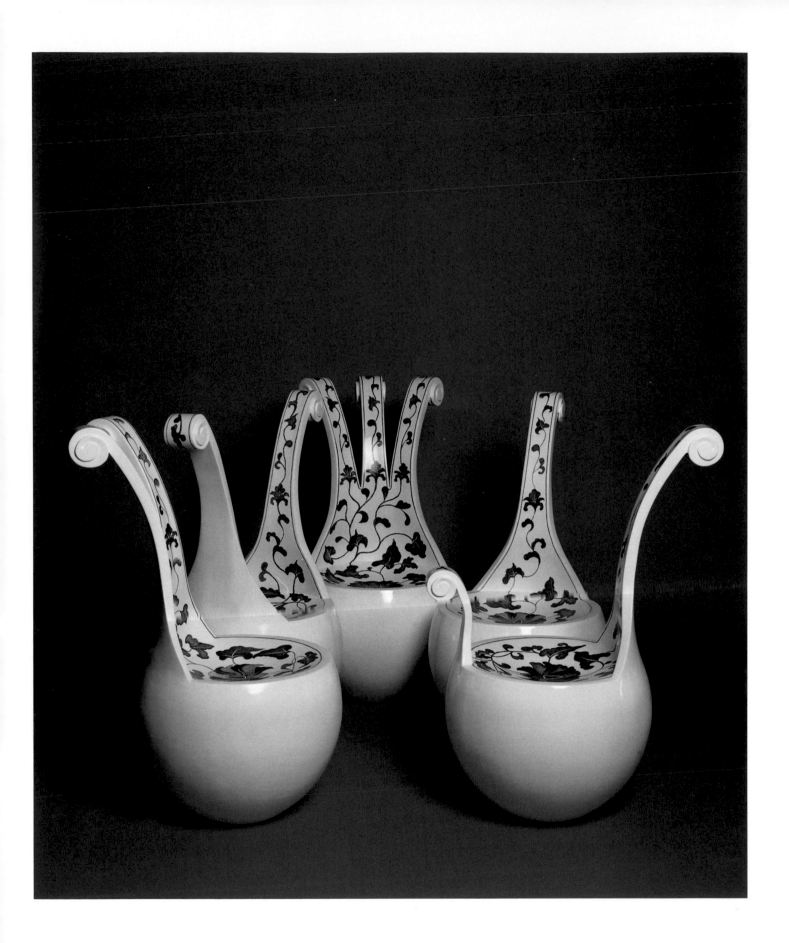

Shao Fan
Contrasts Gallery
<u>Work No. 1 of Year 2006</u>
acrylic, elm
limited edition of 5

Wu Yiming
Contrasts Gallery
<u>Table-Chair</u>
painted wood
limited edition of 2

Campana Brothers
Fernando + Humberto Campana
Multidão Chair, Banquete Chair, Sharks and
Dolphins Banquete
limited edition chairs upholstered with soft toys
Client: Moss Gallery, NY

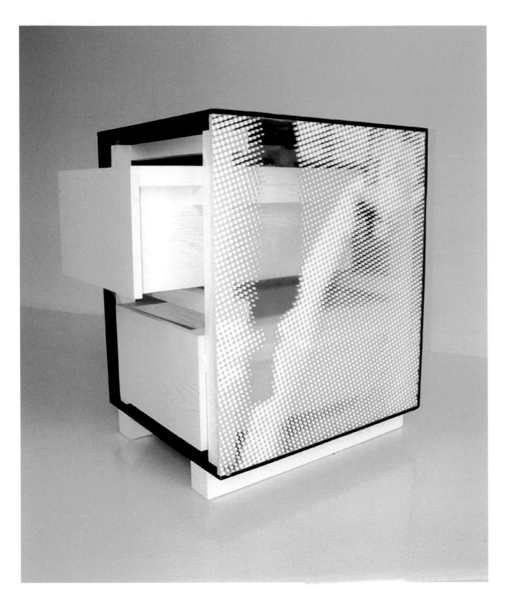

Hella Jongerius
Galerie Kreo
Cupboard #2, Cupboard #6
white lacquered wood and plexiglas one-off,
produced exclusively for Galerie Kreo

Ronan & Erwan Bouroullec
Galerie Kreo
Lit Clos
painted birch plywood, steel, aluminium,
altuglas
Client: Cappellini

-below-
Pierre Charpin
Galerie Kreo
<u>Table Basse "Large DB", "Large R"</u>
brushed and lacquered aluminium table
from the platFORM collection, edition limited
to 8 + 2 artists proofs + 2 prototypes all
numbered and signed
Client: Galerie Kreo

Hella Jongerius
Galerie Kreo
<u>Cupboard #3</u>, <u>#7</u>, <u>#1</u>
white lacquered wood and plexiglas one-off,
produced exclusively for Galerie Kreo

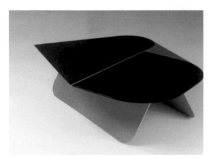

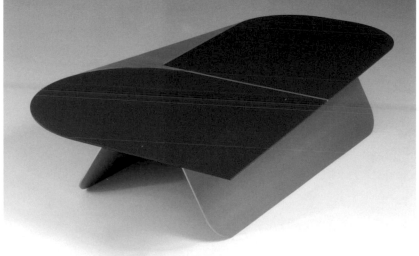

"We need designers to show us how limiting mainstream design is, how narrow the emotional possibilities offered are and how shallow it can be. Design that challenges this reminds us that things could be better if we had the will. There should be some part of the profession dedicated to reflection and design's impact on society."

Anthony Dunne

New parameters and new approaches demand new avenues of enquiry. As well as exploring materials, techniques, niches and narratives in a phase of rapid change such as the one we now find ourselves in, it is also important to question the 'given'.

When, according to Joseph Kosuth, Marcel Duchamp first raised "the function of art as a question" with his Unassisted Readymades, "... art changed its focus from the form of the language to what was being said. Which means that it changed the nature of art from a question of morphology to a question of function"[1] and conceptual art was born. Challenging the fundamental 'given' in this way completely turned art as it was known on its head — or rather turned art towards the head by making the idea behind a work far more important than its execution or visual aspect and thus liberating artists from traditional formats and materials. Conceptual art, in Sol LeWitt's words: "is made to engage the mind of the viewer rather than his eye or emotions",[2] and as such has had a determining effect on the thinking of many artists ever since.

From Duchamp's 1917 'Fountain' (the famous urinal signed 'R.Mutt'), via Joseph Kosuth's 'One and Three Chairs' (comprising a real chair, a photograph of a chair and a dictionary definition of a chair) and Bruce Naumann's 'The Space Underneath My Chair' (a cast of negative space), both from 1965, to the more recent work of Rachael Whitread (including her huge 2005 installation 'Embankment' in London's Tate Modern made from multiple cast interior spaces of cardboard boxes), for example, concept-driven art has had a close affinity and preoccupation with everyday objects. This can involve the spaces that objects do — or do not — occupy; the function of objects (or space) in the expression of an idea and the sense of the execution of that idea, in terms of the 'manufacture' of the artwork itself, being divorced from the conception. There are so many parallels here with design preoccupations that it would be surprising not to see this kind of 'thinking outside the box' being applied in a design context.

The conceptual application of design in addressing issues related to the status quo of contemporary life is a strong feature of the work of British designers Anthony Dunne and Fiona Raby. Dunne + Raby are less concerned with products in the conventional sense and more interested in exploring new roles and contexts for design. Their 'Designs for Fragile Personalities in Anxious Times' project in collaboration with Michael Anastassiades, for example, is a series of products that address contemporary human anxieties about issues such as abduction or nuclear war. The collection includes 'Huggable Atomic Mushrooms' (soft toys shaped like nuclear explosions) and furniture objects with secret cavities for hiding inside. Another series, 'Placebo', features apparent household objects designed to shield owners from, or make them aware of, the invisible electromagnetic waves in their vicinity. Also their 'GPS Table' which displays its exact latitude and longitude co-ordinates on an LCD screen when it has contact to navigation satellites but pronounces itself "lost" when contact is broken, is another good example of conceptual design in this genre. These are clearly not intended to be marketable 'products' as such and are definitely quite different from the limited editions and designer one-offs currently being traded on the fine art market described previously. "For us," says Anthony Dunne, "the real possibilities of conceptual design are not at the furniture/fine art end ... but at the product end, where conceptual design means a parallel world that allows us to ask 'what if?'"

With their collaborative Bootleg Objects project, the German artist Markus Bader and designer Max Wolf began challenging design function in a conceptual way by distorting industrial design archetypes. They took a series of well-known objects and 'bootlegged' them by appropriating the forms and changing the functions. With REBRAUN they changed an iconically utilitarian home sound system, the Audio 1 Kompaktanlage designed by Dieter Rams in 1962, into an MP3 jukebox and server with an added button labelled 'random'. Their RE-BO is a 1973 Bang & Olufsen Beocenter 1400 cassette player adapted to house a smartcard reader, DVD drive and touch screen display, and the radio tuning slide control label now reads 'anything' instead of 'tuning'. The RE-SP is a 1980s Technics SP turntable bereft of all function: the centre pin is gone and the turntable is fixed. Instead of putting on records, one lays 'souvenirs' on the deck such as an image of an old record sleeve fitted with special microchips to play music. To change tracks one has to slap the case with the palm of the hand. Thus "freed from all constraints," say Bader and Wolf, "the record player becomes a nostalgic cult object, the ritual of selecting music turns into aesthetic contemplation and retaining the record sleeves is discerned as a romantic gesture". Bader and Wolf's iconoclastic deconstruction of the design object in this way is an effective method for challenging the given of form and function specifically in revered objects of design that were considered apogees of their genres in their day. By 'bootlegging' them, Bader and Wolf are highlighting the transient nature of design perfection – particularly when it is linked to technology.

The designer Gitta Gschwendtner is also interested in distorting and mutating archetypes. The advantage of a conceptual approach, she says, is that "it subverts the notion of the purpose of design being to industrialise the object". Her 'Furniture Life' objects displayed at the Barrett Marsden gallery in London, in 2006, turn everyday furniture objects into pseudo organisms that have digestive organs and sweat and excrete fluids. Like Steiner and Lenzlinger's environments mentioned in a previous chapter, she too is exploring the weakening borders between the animate and inanimate that design seems to be leading us towards and asking how that will affect our understanding of the object per se.

Some designers experiment with the use of humour to subvert meaning and express ideas and statements visually in the form of ironic inversions. It can be a useful tool to produce shifts in perception by twisting function or lead viewers into uncomfortable territory in order to break down preconceptions, but it is a fine line between gags and one-liners and insightful satire – between kitsch and clever: Are Marcel Wanders' Snot Vases clever Keatsian statements about our precious attitude towards beauty and vases, or schoolboy humour in decorative form? "Humour is very important," says Anthony Dunne, "but it is difficult to work with ... it is a problem when a conceptual design becomes 80% humour and 20% critique; at that point it becomes design entertainment".

It would be a mistake to view these examples of conceptual approaches to design simply as further evidence of cross-discipline thinking, along with the creation of one-offs, hybrids, insertions and introduction of narrative described in previous chapters – although many of them have conceptual elements. Whilst it is obviously vital for designers to work hand in hand with industry and to explore the potential of new technologies, it is just as important for them to be able to disengage from industry in terms of standing back from the process as well. Broadening categories of application brings with it a responsibility to extend critical awareness. Thus designers who concern themselves with non-commercial and speculative products and services and with intangible objects and interfaces are to be welcomed as the pioneers, investigators and researchers in a predominantly consumer-driven field. It is just as important for designers to understand the nature of the things we don't need as the nature of the things that we do.

Barnaby Barford
"Oh please Mummy can we keep it",
"Fuck Off! It's my ball",
"Shit! Now I'm going to be really late"

245

Barnaby Barford
"Told you so!"

Barnaby Barford
Mutton

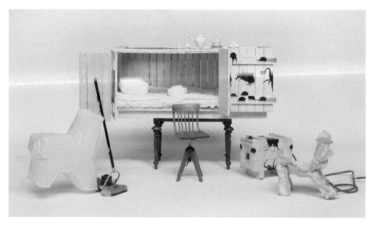

Jurgen Bey
<u>Dustcabinet + Vacuum Cleaner Chair</u>
"An old table and two chairs together with
their sandblasted wooden travelling box form
the dustcabinet. The dustcabinet makes a nice
workspace for a dust researcher.
During the day he works behind his desk
and produces dust. He vacuums the dust into
dust-furniture-bags, which become his soft
pillows to sleep on at night. When he wakes
up, he just has to stick his head out of his
little roofwindow to enjoy a cup of coffee on
top of his cabinet."

-opposite-
<u>Vase-Cupboard-Indian-View</u>
Client: Biennale di Ceramica nell' Arte
Contemporanea Albisola

-opposite-

Peter Marigold
Make/Shift WBP

Gitta Gschwendtner
Slip/Shelf

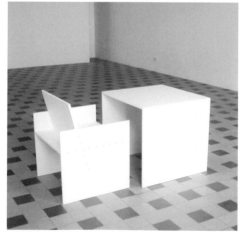

REDESIGNDEUTSCHLAND
Rafael Horzon
Product 250 Workplace 01

REDESIGNDEUTSCHLAND
Rafael Horzon
Product 250 Workplace 01

REDESIGNDEUTSCHLAND
Rafael Horzon + Michel Obladen
<u>Product 1560 Prefabricated House 01</u>
<u>Hausbau</u>
"Hausbau reduces the dream of owning your own place to an absolute minimum. Hausbau makes the dream of owning your own place affordable. Hausbau takes the form of a symmetrical cube with 220 cm edges. Hausbau is easy to set up and take down in a few hours. Hausbau can be used in many ways: outdoors as a minimal flat, mountain hut, garden house, ticket office or kiosk. Indoors as a relaxation booth."

REDESIGNDEUTSCHLAND
Rafael Horzon + Friedrich Killinger
Product 1903 RDD Spiritual Zentrum
"Religions and their misinterpretation are
the biggest causes for crises, irritations and
wars worldwide. For the creation of balance
between all humans, REDESIGNDEUTSCHLAND
proposes the abolition of all religions and
worldwide replacement of all religious
places with Spiritual Zentrums. The Spiritual
Zentrums give space, in the tradition of
enlightenment, for the common development
of strategies and products for a big
community of happy and equal people."

257

Bootlegged 1973 Bang&Olufsen Beocenter
1400 adapted to house a smartcard reader,
DVD drive and touch screen display. The radio
tuning slide control label now reads 'anything'
instead of 'tuning'.

RE-SP
Bootlegged 1980s Technics SP turntable now
apparently bereft of all function: the centre
pin is gone and the turntable is fixed. Instead
of putting on records, one lays 'souvenirs' on
the deck such as an image of an old record
sleeve fitted with special microchips to play
music. To change tracks, one has to slap the
case with the palm of the hand.

Bootleg Objects
Markus Bader + Max Wolf
<u>ReBraun with loudspeaker</u>
Bootlegged Braun Audio 1 stereo system
originally designed by Dieter Rams in 1962
'remixed' into an MP3 jukebox and server with
an added button labelled 'random'.

Dunne + Raby
Anthony Dunne + Fiona Raby
<u>GPS Table</u>
"This table has a global positioning sensor
inside it. It can only display its position in
the world when it has a clear view of the
satellites; the rest of the time it is lost and
indicates this fact. The ideal owner will need
a conservatory or large window, or a garden
so that they can at least bring the table
outdoors from time to time so it can connect
with a satellite and fulfil its potential. We like
the idea that people might feel a little cruel
keeping it indoors."

Dunne + Raby
Anthony Dunne + Fiona Raby
<u>Compass Table</u>
"This table reminds you that electronic
objects extend beyond their visible limits.
The 25 compasses set into its surface twitch
and spin when objects like mobile phones
or laptop computers are placed on it. The
twitching needles can be interpreted as being
either sinister or charming, depending on the
viewer's state of mind. When we designed the
compass table, we wondered if a neat-freak
might try to make all the needles line up,
ignoring the architectural space of the room
in favour of the Earth's magnetic field."

Jason Miller Studio
Kids Have No Respect

Gitta Gschwendtner
Chaise with Guts
installation at Barrett Marsden Gallery,
London

Dunne + Raby
Anthony Dunne + Fiona Raby

Nipple Chair

"An electric field sensor and antenna are mounted beneath the seat of the chair. When the chair is placed in an electromagnetic field, two nipples set into the back start to vibrate, and the sitter is made aware of the radio waves penetrating their torso. It is up to them whether they stay and enjoy the gentle buzz, or move to a 'quieter' spot. As fields can also flow up through the sitter's body from electric wiring running underneath the floor, the chair has footrests so that you can isolate your feet from the ground. We like that it is slightly anthropomorphic; it's as though you are sitting on its lap."

Electro-Draught Excluder

"This object is a classic placebo. Though the draught excluder is made from conductive foam, it is not grounded, and therefore does not really absorb radiation. We were interested in whether or not it would make the owner feel more comfortable. If you are working near a TV, for example, you might place the object between you and the TV to create a sort of shadow — a comfort zone where you simply feel better."

Dunne + Raby
Anthony Dunne + Fiona Raby
<u>Huggable Atomic Mushroom</u>
from Designs for Fragile Personalities in
Anxious Times; A Collection of Prescription
Products with Michael Anastassiades

INDEX

INDEX

INDEX

INDEX

References

page 7: Gaetano Pesce, quoted by Lyle Rexer,
One from the Heart, DAMn magazine No. 8
Oct/Nov 2006

page 38: Nicolas Cage, Wild at Heart,
by David Lynch, 1990

page 72: Kory Towska, Lüstige Blätter,
vol. 14 pub. Berlin, 1899, trans. Jeffery Howe

page 116: Jurgen Bey
from: www.vividvormgeving.nl

page 180: Gerhard Seltmann + Werner Lippert
Entry Paradise: New Worlds of Design,
Ed. G. Seltman, W. Lippert, Birkhäuser, 2006

page 224: Brad Holland
from: www.newyorkartworld.com

page 242: Anthony Dunne
interview with Sophie Lovell, December 2006

Footnotes

page 242:
[1] Joseph Kosuth, Art after Philosophy, first pub.
Studio International, vol. 178, nos. 915-17,
London 1969

[2] Sol Le-Witt, Paragraphs on Conceptual Art,
Art Forum, 1967

FURNISH

Furniture and Interior Design for the 21st Century

Texts written by Sophie Lovell
Edited by Robert Klanten, Sophie Lovell and Birga Meyer

Layout and design by Birga Meyer for dgv
Project management by Julian Sorge for dgv

Production management by Vinzenz Geppert
Proofreading by English Express

Thanks to Barbara Glasner, Andrej Kupetz and Christian Maith

Cover motif:
"Alquimista" ceiling lamp with "Têtes" by Robert Stadler; photo by Patrick Gries

Back Cover motifs:
"'Mountain Rescue' Kebab Lamp" by Clare + Harry Richardson
"Model Ideas" by Industreal; photo by Pol!femo
"Blow-Void 3" by Ron Arad; photo by Erik Hesmerg
"Inner Beauty" by Guðrún Lilja Gunnlaugsdóttir
"Waternetworks Exhibition" by Yves Fidalgo + Cédric Decroux;
photo by Geoffrey Cottenceau
"Shelflife" by Charles Trevelyan; photo by George Ong

Printed by Graphicom Srl., Italy
Made in Europe

Published by Die Gestalten Verlag, Berlin 2007
ISBN: 978-3-89955-176-1

None of the content in this book was published in exchange for payment by
commercial parties or designers; dgv selected all included work based solely
on its artistic merit.

For more information please check: www.die-gestalten.de

Respect copyright – encourage creativity!

Bibliographic information published by Die Deutsche Bibliothek.
Die Deutsche Bibliothek lists this publication in the Deutsche Nationalbibliografie;
detailed bibliographic data is available in the Internet at http://dnb.ddb.de.